Earth Bible Commentary

Series Editor
Norman C. Habel

RUTH

An Earth Bible Commentary

Alice Mary Sinnott RSM

LONDON · NEW YORK · OXFORD · NEW DELHI · SYDNEY

T&T CLARK
Bloomsbury Publishing Plc
50 Bedford Square, London, WC1B 3DP, UK
1385 Broadway, New York, NY 10018, USA

BLOOMSBURY, T&T CLARK and the T&T Clark logo are trademarks of
Bloomsbury Publishing Plc

First published in Great Britain 2020

Cover design: Charlotte James
Cover image © borchee/istock

A catalogue record for this book is available from the British Library.

Library of Congress Cataloging-in-Publication Data
Names: Sinnott, Alice M., author.
Title: Ruth : an Earth Bible commentary / Alice M. Sinnott.
Description: New York : T&T CLark, 2020. | Series: Earth Bible commentary |
Includes bibliographical references and index. | Summary: "Alice Sinnott
highlights ecological dimensions of the Book of Ruth and shows how the
narrator gives voice to the way in which the Earth functions throughout
the story. Sinnott considers non-human characters as legitimate
determining factors in the structuring of the narrative and recognizes
Earth and members of the Earth community as valid subjects in the
narrative. Integral to Sinnott's reading of the text is a concern for
Earth and matters such as food, famine, death, harvests, grain, day and
night and members of the Earth community"– Provided by publisher.
Identifiers: LCCN 2020012529 (print) | LCCN 2020012530 (ebook) |
ISBN 9780567676221 (hardback) | ISBN 9780567676238 (pdf) |
ISBN 9780567695468 (epub)
Subjects: LCSH: Bible. Ruth–Criticism, interpretation, etc. |
Human ecology in the Bible. | Nature in the Bible.
Classification: LCC BS1315.52 .S58 2020 (print) | LCC BS1315.52 (ebook) |
DDC 222/.3507–dc23
LC record available at https://lccn.loc.gov/2020012529
LC ebook record available at https://lccn.loc.gov/2020012530

ISBN: HB: 978-0-5676-7622-1
ePDF: 978-0-5676-7623-8
ePUB: 978-0-5676-9546-8

Typeset by Newgen KnowledgeWorks Pvt. Ltd., Chennai, India

To find out more about our authors and books visit www.bloomsbury.com
and sign up for our newsletters.

Dedicated to the memory of my parents, Robert and Annie Sinnott

CONTENTS

ABBREVIATIONS

ABD	*Anchor Bible Dictionary*
AH	*Artibus et Historiae*
AYBRIL	Anchor Yale Bible Reference Library
BBR	*Bulletin of Biblical Research*
BDB	*Brown Driver and Briggs*
BibInt	*Biblical Interpretation Series*
BS	*Bibliotheca Sacra*
BTB	*Brown Driver and Brigs*
BZAW	Beihefte zur Zeitschrift für altestamentliche Wissenschaft
CBQ	*Catholic Biblical Quarterly*
HBT	*Horizons in Biblical Theology*
HSM	*Harvard Semitic Monographs*
HTKAT	Herders Theologische Kommentar zum Alten Testament
JBL	*Journal of Biblical Literature*
JCT	*Journal of Constructive Theology*
JPS	*Jewish Publication Society*
JSOT	*Journal for the Study of the Old Testament*
JSOTSup	*Journal for the Study of the Old Testament Supplement Series*
LT	*Literature and Theology*
NIB	*New Interpreters Bible*
NRSV	*New Revised Standard Version Bible*
OTE	*Old Testament Essays*
OTL	Old Testament Library
SBL	Society of Biblical Literature
VT	*Vetus Testamentum*
WBC	Word Biblical Commentary
ZAW	*Zeitschrift für die Altestamentliche Wissenschsft*

Chapter 1

INTRODUCTION

"Wherever you go, I will go … ," an excerpt from the favourite text from the book of Ruth, has been the chosen reading at numerous weddings I have attended. Interestingly it is only at weddings that I hear sermons, homilies, and reflections on Ruth's vow to Naomi, her mother-in-law. The Ruth story continues to be a favourite Bible story for many Jews and Christians. In the Christian canons, the book of Ruth sits among books portraying war, battles, trickery, treachery, abominable violence, bloodshed, brutal reprisals, and total disregard for the Torah. So the Ruth story, when read in this context, raises many questions about how such a human story appears in such horrific literary company. The simplicity and attractiveness of the book of Ruth as a human story masks the pivotal roles that Earth and the Earth community, day, night, land, fields, barley harvest, wheat harvest, and threshing play in the story. Over the centuries, many have read the book of Ruth as a consoling story of how human beings can treat others, outsiders, and insiders with ḥesed "loving kindness." It is the perspective of this commentary that such a reading reflects some understanding of what it means to be an Earth person and to respect and honour Earth creatures and elements. Care and concern for others demands that human beings step outside and beyond what one considers minimum, primary human responsibility, and to seek greater wholeness in the Earth community.

Scholars have generally overlooked Earth and Earth creatures in the Ruth story. Positive assessments of the story capture broad reading audiences and studies. Potentially harmful features of the narrative have created many ethical and theological difficulties for some modern readers; some have even disputed the worth of this story in contemporary society. The text itself addresses significant difficulties along the way and eventually presents a more positive assessment.

Difficulties with the story are not limited to theological and legal issues, however. They begin with debates over classic topics such as date of composition, purpose, and authorship. The presentation of these matters will be relatively brief since they are informative but finally not decisive for assessing the significance of reading the Ruth narrative from an Earth perspective.

Date and purpose

Christian traditions set the Ruth story historically by its opening line in the era of the Judges and conclusion with mentions of King David. Thus, many scholars have argued that the composition appears to be from the time of David or later. Critical scholarship in the first half of the twentieth century proposed that the book was from the time of Ezra and Nehemiah some 550 years after the reign of David. Arguments for this date rest primarily on linguistic and grammatical features such as expressions that appear to show the influence of the Aramaic language on the Hebrew of Ruth, influences that were thought to be only possible in the post-exilic period when Aramaic became the dominant spoken language. Ruth is not a polemical text. While Deut 23:4–9 and Neh 13:1–3 display hostility towards Moabites, Ruth does not. Concerns about inclusion/exclusion, genealogical purity, and inclusion of foreign women to marriage do appear. The worship of YHWH does pose concerns, particularly in Isaiah 55–66. Ruth's vow to Naomi includes "your God will be my God, too." However, her loyalty appears to be primarily to Naomi herself. The main argument for a post-exilic dating is that the book engages with a post-exilic issue regarding the inclusion of foreigners, while Israelites must always have struggled with the problem of "foreigners." Their self-understanding included their history of being exiles/migrants in Egypt – the Torah commanded that they treat foreigners well (Lev 19:33–34). The narrative is independent of the references to a historical period, and its geography is similarly independent. Ruth has a self-contained landscape. The story begins in Bethlehem, moves in three verses to Moab, returns to Bethlehem of Judah, and remains there. Just because a book is relevant in the post-exilic period does not mean that was the time of its origin. Reworking already existing narratives may not have been unusual in the light of shifting realities. Earlier elements remained, but a reinterpretation gave the narrative new meaning. Many scholars date all or most of Ruth to the post-exilic period, and this study agrees with the arguments for this dating.[1]

Genealogies in Ruth

This commentary dates the Hebrew text well into the exilic or even post-exilic period. The original purpose of the story may have been to support claims of the

---

1. See Frederic W. Bush, *Ruth-Esther*, WBC (Dallas, TX: Word Books, 1996), 30; Ziony Zevit, "Dating Ruth: Legal, Linguistic and Historical Observations," *ZAW* 117 (2005): 574–600; Edward F. Campbell, *Ruth: A New Translation with Introduction and Commentary*, Anchor Bible (Garden City, NY: Doubleday, 1975), 26–27; Tamara Eskenazi and Tikva Frymer-Kensky, *The JPS Bible Commentary: Ruth* (Philadelphia, PA: Jewish Publication Society of America, 2011), xvi–xix; Alice L. Laffey and Mahri Leonard-Fleckman, *Ruth: Wisdom Commentary*, ed. Barbara E. Reid, vol. 8 (Collegeville, MN: Liturgical Press, 2017), lix–lxi.

Davidic line as it points to David with the mention of Ephrathah in the opening verses (1:2) and at its closing (4:11). Also there is a twofold mention of David in the narrative conclusion (4:17) and in the longer genealogy (4:18–22). Some debate the antiquity of the genealogy and the direction of likely literary dependence between the concluding genealogy in Ruth and the parallel information in 1 Chr 2. There is much to dispute concerning the two genealogies, and some scholars consider each version to have an independent primary source. Regardless of which view seems most likely, the genealogy used in Ruth is a stylized and precise form. Boaz holds the seventh place of note in traditional genealogies, and David holds the tenth and final place.[2] The number of names is certainly insufficient to cover a human time frame from Perez to David in the biblical tradition. Within the genealogy, the names of Ram and Salmon are highly problematic as they lack any other attestation beyond the parallel in 1 Chronicles and have different spelling in the Hebrew Bible. Oddly, the genealogy begins with Perez rather than with his father Judah, the eponymous ancestor. Nielsen suggests that court scribes prepared the genealogy for propaganda purposes. If this is correct, why did the genealogy not begin with Judah? Ruth 4:12 names the ancestor of the tribe of Judah and omits Ram and Salmon, thus continuing the seventh and tenth places for Boaz and David. Certainly, the issues surrounding the genealogy are complex and beyond the scope of this commentary.

View of foreigners/outsiders

A starting point for this commentary is the narrator's subtle instruction concerning the community's view of outsiders. David is the narrator's means of legitimating an inclusive attitude towards foreigners, especially towards foreign women. The Ruth story encourages Israelites to accept gifts of care and concern from outsiders while they likewise must extend their care and concern beyond the boundaries of the bloodlines of the covenant community. An earlier emphasis on challenging the limitations of traditional ethnic barriers might have had relevance in the eras of Ezra and Nehemiah. The community might have heard the story as a challenge to the purity perspectives of the late pre-exilic Deuteronomistic History with its warnings against relationships with the local Canaanites. It might have addressed in story form the tensions arising early in the post-exilic era between Jewish returnees from Babylon and those who had remained in the land after the fall of Jerusalem. Noting the repeated need to challenge narrow exclusivism in the life of the ancient community should remind readers that the story of Ruth addresses a perennial issue in human communities. The question put to Jesus, "And who is

---

2. The number ten figures prominently in the Ruth narrative, for example, Ruth 1:4; ten years in Moab, 4:2; ten elders as witnesses at the gate, 4:2; ten-name genealogy in 4:18–22. In the symbolic significance of numbers in Scripture, ten is the number signifying divine order.

my neighbour?" that elicited from Jesus the story of the good Samaritan (Luke 10:29) addresses this same debate about the limits of neighbourliness. Who are the faithful ones in the community and how far should the boundaries for exercising genuine concern extend? For ancient readers/hearers of Ruth who recognized and revered the legitimacy of David's kingship, the references to David could function as an endorsement making its controversial claims binding upon them. Perhaps the story encouraged them to recognize the need for care and concern for outsiders and how they might extend their care and concern beyond the boundaries of the bloodlines of the covenant community. While an emphasis on challenging the limitations of traditional ethnic barriers might have had relevance in the eras of Ezra and Nehemiah, it is not necessary that the story was composed only at that time in order to bear the didactic intent of a word about inclusion.

Eco-justice hermeneutic principles

Norman Habel in his preface to *The Birth, the Curse, and the Greening of Earth: An Ecological Reading of Genesis 1-11* summarizes the fundamental hermeneutical principles that guide an Earth reading of the book of Ruth.[3] These principles of intrinsic worth, interconnectedness, voice, purpose, mutual custodianship, and resistance offer a way of engaging the Ruth story with a hermeneutic of suspicion, identification, and retrieval. Anthropocentric texts usually ignore the Earth's presence in the text. Readers may struggle at first to recognize Earth, Earth creatures, and Earth elements in the story of Ruth and to retrieve the Earth presences, particularly when they seem not to be the author's explicit narrative focus. The interpretive hermeneutic of suspicion, identification, and retrieval offers a way of hearing the Ruth story afresh. The narrative involves Earth, Earth creatures, and Earth elements. The four main eco-justice principles that guide this study are intrinsic worth, interconnectedness, voice, and mutual custodianship.

Reading Ruth from an Earth perspective

A stated aim of the Earth Bible series is to "recognise Earth not simply as a topic to be explored in the text but also as a subject in the text with which we seek to relate empathetically."[4] An Earth reading of the book of Ruth requires consideration of primary literary units that scholars have traditionally identified in this short story. The study examines the literary structure of sections of the story and Earth themes and tropes throughout the complete narrative. This investigation of sections of the

---

3. Norman C. Habel, *The Birth, the Curse and the Greening of Earth: An Ecological Reading of Genesis 1–11* (Sheffield: Sheffield Phoenix Press, 2011), 1–16.

4. Norman C. Habel, *Readings from the Perspective of Earth*, ed. Normal C. Habel, Earth Bible, vol. 1 (Sheffield: Sheffield Academic Press, 2000), 37.

narrative and how the story builds to a resolution will consider the presence of Earth, Earth characters, and Earth components as legitimate determining factors in the structuring of the narrative. Appropriate references to studies by a variety of biblical scholars may illustrate recent studies of Ruth. This study recognizes Earth, Earth spaces and settings, members of the Earth community, and Earth creatures as valid subjects. The design of the narrative will highlight dimensions of the text that have been ignored or dismissed in the past, but which demand special attention in a reading of the narrative from an Earth perspective. This study will consider how the narrator represents and gives voice to how Earth, domains of Earth, and members of the Earth community function throughout the story. As Habel so emphatically states, the "preferred approach is one that moves beyond a focus on ecological themes to a process of listening to and identifying with the Earth as a presence or voice in the text."[5]

Analysis of plot, characters, and text

An analysis of the plot, the characters, and the meaning of the text flows from the structural design of the narrative. Close examination of textual units as coherent units of plot demands consideration of typical anthropocentric and dualistic readings of the text by past scholars. Such a search may reveal some limitations of various approaches, but this study will not engage in lengthy dialogue with the numerous interpreters of this narrative. Integral to a study of the Ruth text will be empathy and concern for Earth as such, for domains of Earth such as famine, death, harvests, grain, day, night, water, land, human and non-human lives in the Earth community. The study seeks to identify the significance of the actions embarked on by Earth, Earth creatures, and Earth characters who are subjects but also active in the plot and the narrative. Of interest is whether the storyteller makes specific roles and characters convincing. By identifying with Earth and all its various elements, actors, and voices in the narrative, this study seeks to read the text with new eyes and to discern previously overlooked dimensions in it.

This study aims to consider and unearth nuances of meaning in word plays, rhetorical innuendoes, intertextual associations, mythic dimensions, and cultural imagery. By giving special attention to how the narrator depicts Earth and Earth creatures, the study aims to discover subjects that warrant reflexion in terms of the environment of the text. While attending to connections that scholars have traditionally made with symbols, concepts, and language from cultural contexts of the ancient Near East, their viability in terms of an ecological hermeneutic is paramount.

At crucial points, the study moves from the analysis of specific words, images, and textual units to focus on the broader ecological patterns and issues that

---

5. Norman C. Habel, *The Birth, the Curse and the Greening of Earth: An Ecological Reading of Genesis 1-11* (Sheffield: Sheffield Phoenix Press, 2011), 1–2.

emerge. Of paramount concern in this study is the narrative and how Earth, light, darkness, visibility, field, food, water, famine, and harvests feature in the narrative. The study focuses on reading the articulated, implied, or concealed language of the narrative from an Earth perspective. Such a reading employs an ecological hermeneutic of suspicion, identification, and retrieval.

Retrieval of Earth's voices

Attempts to identify with and understand the Earth and elements of the Earth community require a search to retrieve dimensions of the Ruth text that earlier scholars have ignored or dismissed as irrelevant. This study seeks to identify Earth and Earth elements in the Ruth text and to attend to factors informing the meaning of the narrative. In the act of retrieval, the study seeks to hear the voices of the non-human characters in the story. The reconstruction of non-human voices is as legitimate as the efforts of scholars in the past who sought to reconstruct the social, historical, or cultural world of the narrator/author from clues embedded in the text. Here the study uses textual clues to hear Earth and Earth creatures and voices in and through the narrative and to discern the suppressed voices of oppressed non-human characters within the text. As key characters relate the narrative from new perspectives, readers may gain a richer appreciation of the values once associated with Earth and Earth creatures that twenty-first-century readers may have lost. Such awareness may highlight some of the injustices that the Earth, Earth elements, and Earth domains have experienced at the hands of humans and other Earth creatures in the Ruth narrative. The voices of Earth and her creatures may utter cries for justice that readers today must heed.

Literary forms and structure

This study recognizes the importance of the literary forms encompassed in the Ruth narrative. The first and most significant genre is that of the short story. The Hebrew short story uses "artistic and elevated prose containing rhythmic elements which are poetic," takes an interest in typical people, and seeks to both entertain and instruct.[6] Especially relevant: they look at regular events as being the scene of God's subtly providential activity. Some introductory comments about the short story appear in this introduction and these are further developed in more detail at appropriate points in the commentary. An interest in Celtic myths and folklore has enabled me to appreciate that stories are not simple explanations of reality, but powerful expressions of the interconnection between humans, Earth, and the Earth community. Some characteristics of the Celtic myths also appear in the Ruth story, especially the notion of a primordial power from the distant

---

6. Campbell, *Ruth*, 5.

past that persists in the present. Human beings have a spiritual force connected with their place of birth, their ancestors, and geographical Earth of origin. This study will consider sites in the Ruth landscape that connect with familiar Bible stories. A Celtic story may, for example, revolve around a great ancestor such as Cuchulainn, Brian Boru, the Wild Geese, or more recently the Croppies, the Great Famine, and the Easter Rising. Peoples of many lands treasure similar narratives. They illustrate how human beings who live with stories as part of their world of meaning have a physical, social, and spiritual affinity and connection with Earth and Earth creatures. Likewise, the Ruth narrative reflects an inexplicable connection with Earth. Many scholars have searched the world of stories originating from narratives about death-defying survival. Underlying many ancient and more recent stories are catastrophe narratives that feature an Earth crisis regarding climate, food supply, or water supply that can only be averted by phenomenal or divine intervention. The outcome of such a cataclysm may have resulted in permanent changes in how survivors organized their society. Underpinning such a narrative may be an explanation for how things are in the present. There may be a sense of gratitude or even uniqueness as being oppressed or resilient in the face of injustice or catastrophe.

Earth themes and design

This Earth reading of Ruth considers the Earth themes that flow through the narrative. Each chapter will examine how the themes emerge and how the Earth, Earth creatures, and Earth elements pervade the literary structure of the narrative. An investigation of the design will consider non-human characters and components as legitimate determining factors in the structuring of the story. Where appropriate, the study draws on a typical structural analysis exercise to identify the anthropocentric bias typical of many such analyses in the past. This study aims to recognize Earth, domains of Earth, and members and elements of the Earth community as valid subjects in the examination of the narrative. As a result, the design of the narrative may highlight dimensions of the text that scholars have ignored or dismissed in the past, but which demand special attention when reading the narrative from an Earth perspective. In this context, the study will attempt to identify possible literary sources of the text. The study will not pursue a form-critical or tradition-critical analysis. Instead, the concern here will be to identify how the narrator and other speaking characters in Ruth represent and give voice to Earth, domains of Earth, and members of the Earth community.

Analysis

An analysis of the plot, the characters, and meaning of the text will flow from the structural design of the narrative in the preceding section. The study will examine textual units as intelligible elements of the plot. This analysis will consider essential anthropocentric and dualistic readings of the text by past scholars that may illustrate the drawbacks of some approaches but will not engage in lengthy dialogue with the many interpreters of this story. Integral to an Earth reading of the text is an empathetic orientation and concern for Earth and creatures of the Earth community, such as light, darkness, earth, water, fields, food crops, seasons, famine, harvests, and much more. The task is to ascertain how the narrator depicts roles the human and non-human characters play in the plot and the development of the narrative. By identifying with these non-human characters in the narrative, readers may see the text with new eyes and may discern dimensions that they might otherwise overlook. This study carefully considers the nuances of meaning found in the use of key terms, word plays, rhetorical innuendoes, intertextual associations, and cultural imagery. By paying attention to how the author of Ruth has depicted the Earth of the narrative, the study seeks to allow Earth creatures and actors from that world to emerge. The study examines, from an Earth perspective, symbols, concepts, and language from the cultural contexts of the world of the ancient Near East. At critical points, this will necessitate a move from the analysis of specific words, images, and textual units to a focus on the broader Earth patterns and issues that may emerge. While knowledge of the biblical languages and the ancient Near Eastern context supports the study, the publication does not require readers to be familiar with the original forms of biblical expressions and narrative tropes. By focusing on the language of the narrative and implied or hidden meaning, this work seeks to read, from the perspectives of Earth, its creatures and elements by employing the ecological hermeneutics of suspicion, identification, and retrieval.

Retrieval

By identifying and empathizing with Earth and members of the Earth community, a preliminary analysis will seek to retrieve dimensions of the text that have been ignored or dismissed. The study seeks to locate readers within the various environments in Ruth and recognize factors and forces that inform the meaning of the text. In retrieval mode, readers seek to identify voices of Earth and members of the Earth community. The reconstruction of these voices, one could argue, is as legitimate as scholars in the past who sought to reconstruct social, historical, or cultural worlds of authors from clues embedded in the text. This study uses textual clues to free Earth and Earth creatures to relate the story from a non-human perspective and conscious of the human audience. To discern suppressed voices of oppressed non-human characters in the text, one must read against the grain. Readers who do so may gain an appreciation of the values revealed. When the narrative speaks from an Earth perspective, the voices of Earth and Earth creatures alert readers to the many injustices that the Earth and Earth creatures have experienced at the hands of humans and Earth catastrophes. The voice of Earth and her multitude of creatures become a chorus crying out for justice that readers must attempt to heed.

Earth themes

Famine, a natural cause of the tragedy, launches a series of increasingly painful events in the Earth realm that combine to establish one of the two primary motifs in the first act. The first motif is emptiness. First Elimelech dies (1:3), leaving Naomi and her two sons. The two sons die (v. 5) leaving Naomi with her two widowed Moabite daughters-in-law. Finally, she persuades one daughter-in-law, Orpah, to return to her mother's house in Moab, so Ruth insists on remaining with Naomi (v.18), whose descent into a state of "emptiness" took ten years (v. 4). The narrator covers the downward spiral in eighteen verses (1:1–18). The remainder of the narrative covers perhaps three months from the beginning to the end of both the barley harvest and the wheat harvest (1:22–2:23).

Famine is a perfect archetype at this point in the narrative as it introduces the concept of physical barrenness. The Earth was barren, unfruitful, empty. The concept of barrenness moves to the private realm when the reader realizes that Ruth and Orpah are both barren (1:5; 4:13).

The book of Judges provides the historical setting for the events of Ruth. The narrator invites comparison with the era of Judges (Ruth 1:1). A story such as the account of the Levite, from Ephraim, who retrieved his concubine from Bethlehem, her home (Judg 19:1) to which she had returned (v. 2). They left Bethlehem to return to Ephraim. Tragedy befell them. Benjaminites raped and killed the concubine and killed her husband. In retaliation, Israelites slaughtered all but six hundred Benjaminites. However, to ensure the continuation of the tribe of Benjamin, the survivors captured young women from Shiloh and Jabesh-Gilead to serve as wives for the surviving Benjaminites in order to ensure the continuation of the tribe of Benjamin. Such a horrific story contrasts sharply with the Ruth narrative. Ruth 1:1–5 sketches tragic Earth events, and their long-term consequences following Elimelech's departure from Bethlehem.

Following verse 5, the "return" motif appears with the announcement that the Lord has visited his people and given them food (v. 6). Ruth's reply to Naomi (1:16–17) suggest a peaceful resolution of the Ruth narrative as the provision of food after famine assures Naomi of YHWH's faithfulness and prompts her to return to Bethlehem. Naomi is barren; she has lost her husband, her two sons, and Orpah. Even Ruth's vow of *ḥeseḏ* (vv. 16–17) seems to anticipate a tragic end with its final focus on death and burial: "Where you die, I will die … There I will be buried." Verses 1-18 introduce and develop the "emptiness" motif. However, the motif leading chapter one is "return." This first act spans all the tragic consequences as well as the experience (vv. 19–22b). For a return home, one must have an initial departure. Ruth 1:1–5 outlines the family's departure and the immediate repercussions. The "return" motif appears in verse 6 when Naomi decides to "return" home to Bethlehem.

There is further cause for hope when Naomi and Ruth emerge from a winter of barrenness into a potentially fruitful spring. They arrived in Bethlehem as the barley harvest was beginning. Seasonal notes play a subtle but distinctive role in the development of the narrative in Ruth. Autumn and winter are noticeable only in the arrival of Naomi and Ruth, as this turning point coincides with their arrival at the beginning of the barley harvest in April when winter had ended. Their arrival at the beginning of the barley harvest was more than coincidence.

The import of spring extends beyond a literary expression of hope for a fruitful land to the association of the barley harvest with the festivals celebrated at that time of year, particularly Passover, Unleavened Bread, and First Fruits (Lev 23:4–14).

Naomi: An existence devoid of joy

Naomi indicates that she sees her life as an existence devoid of joy. She asks to be called Mara (bitter) in verse 20. Here all the harmful elements are present in concentrated form. It is as if this is the unpleasant face of Earth and the Earth's elements. Verses 20–22a form the nadir of the narrative. Naomi and Ruth are now physically present in Bethlehem, and Naomi seems to foresee herself living out her remaining days in bitterness and recounts her reasons for bitterness. "The Almighty has dealt very bitterly with me" (v. 20). YHWH allowed her to leave Bethlehem "full" (of hope, love, family, purpose) but had brought her back "empty" (v. 21). Naomi's bitterness and emptiness typify the famine that has typified the nation in the time of the Judges and reflected the Earth famine that physically afflicted the land, destroying the harvests. The scene ends with a narrative bracket emphasizing the theme of "return": So Naomi returned together with Ruth the Moabite, her daughter-in-law, who came back with her from the country of Moab. They came to Bethlehem at the beginning of the barley harvest (Ruth 1:22). This repetition mirrors the double statement of Naomi's return with her daughter-in-law, which closed out the first scene (1:6–7). The third scene in Ruth 1:19b–22a portrays Naomi and Ruth as they arrived in Bethlehem (v. 19) and caused a stir.[7]

---

7. Campbell, *Ruth*, 75.

Chapter 2

RUTH AND NAOMI: WIDOWS AND MIGRANTS

The Ruth story opens in Bethlehem where hunger, starvation, and famine drive Elimelech, Naomi, and their sons Mahlon and Chilion into exile to Moab, a land, along with its inhabitants, traditionally considered to be at enmity with Israel (Ruth 1:1–2). In Moab, death claims Elimelech and leaves Naomi a widow. The sons take Moabite wives, Orpah and Ruth (1:4), but this promise of new life vanishes when death and sterility take centre stage with the deaths of Mahlon and Chilion, thus also reducing Ruth and Orpah to widowhood. Now the three widows must decide their next move. Death and barrenness, the life-defying events outlined in Ruth 1:1–5, suggest a human story without a future (cf. 4:14–17).[1] With the three male characters interred in the fields of Moab, Naomi decides to return to the land of Judah because "she had heard that the Lord had visited his people and given them food." This choice signals a new beginning (lātē lāhem lāhem) with a return to her land of Bethlehem. The news that the land of Judah is again fruitful prompts Naomi's decision that follows.[2]

Ruth's dramatic vow to accompany Naomi in life and death (Ruth 1:16–17) to a foreign land is an Earth-centred decision. She undertakes to become one with the Earth of Judah, Naomi's land. "So, Naomi returned together with Ruth the Moabite, her daughter-in-law, who came back with her from the country of Moab" (1:22). Ruth is willing to adopt the land of Judah, Naomi's land, as her home. Auspiciously fruitful Earth welcomes the women as their arrival in Bethlehem coincides with the beginning of the barley harvest. Ruth 1:22 alerts readers to the significance of the Earth's seasons and produce by highlighting how Earth and Earth's activities lead and guide the actions of the human characters. From an Earth perspective, the first chapter of Ruth moves from famine in 1:1 to fruitful

---

1. The death of the sons Mahlon and Chilion at the story's beginning is counterbalanced at the end by the birth of a son who holds the promise of a future, not only for the family at the centre of the narrative but for the nation of Israel also (4:14–17).

2. This is the first of just two references to God's direct intervention in Earth fruitfulness. In both instances, YHWH acts to secure a future, first by the provision of food and second by enabling the conception of a child (4:13). In the Ruth narrative, YHWH is the source of blessing—"may YHWH deal kindly with you" (v. 8) and Shaddai, the Almighty, of catastrophe "the Almighty has dealt bitterly with me" (v. 20).

harvest in 1:22 and from the land of Bethlehem to the land of Moab and back to the land of Bethlehem.

Festivals in Ruth

The feast of Pentecost linked with the end of barley and wheat harvests will be discussed in greater detail in later chapters. The festive cycle in Israel corresponded to specific points on the agricultural calendar, which also happened to reinforce the emptiness and fullness motifs as developed in Ruth. There is no direct mention of any of these feasts in the book of Ruth. However, how does a reader deal with the pointed seasonal references in 1:22 and 2:23 as just seasonal references? Do the prominent agricultural images of famine, harvest, wheat, and barley serve no purpose other than to reinforce metaphorical parallels with the main characters? Maybe they and other such references are subtle artistic devices that draw attention to the significance of the feasts that lies beyond the surface observations. Maybe the lack of explicit mention of the feasts in the narrative is an indirect indication binding the artistic motif to the lives of the characters emphasizing the blessing of YHWH who made fruitful what had been barren.

The study will examine these three feasts briefly here as they relate to the development of the structure of the book of Ruth. At Passover, the Israelites celebrated their liberation from slavery, and the faithfulness of YHWH in bringing them to the land promised to Abraham (Gen 12, 15). Ruth too had come from a foreign land to the land of promise just in time for the celebration of this feast. The Feast of Unleavened Bread focused on the Israelites' willingness to cut themselves off from their old life in Egypt. Leaven in the context of this feast symbolizes continuity. It was a symbol of the connection with the old life of slavery. In calling for the baking of unleavened bread, YHWH was calling for a symbolic break with the past life of slavery.

Similarly, Ruth broke with her early life in Moab when she decided to accompany Naomi into whatever future lay ahead. Ruth made her decision at the same time of year that Israel had decided to leave Egypt. Her break was not less complete but, centuries apart through her loss and grief, might have been more intense. She left family, home, and traditions to live in a foreign land and make her God a foreign god! Moreover, she joined a destitute widow as her travelling companion not as a Moses figure!

Perhaps the most significant of these feasts for this study considering the agricultural motif is the Feast of First Fruits where the wave offering of a sheaf of freshly harvested barley signified the Israelites' recognition of their need for divine provision (Lev 23:11). Readers would have recognized the significance of Ruth gleaning among sheaves of barley at the very time Israelites celebrated a feast that focused on the nations' need for Divine provision. Moreover, this is not to overlook Naomi's earlier request to YHWH to deal kindly with Ruth and Orpah, that is, give them husbands, homes, and security (Ruth 1:8–9). It is puzzling that Naomi did not see herself as in need of Divine provision, or is she expressing a notion that she is beyond the point of receiving help from the Lord (v. 13)? Resenting her lot in life, Naomi appears to foster a fatalistic forbearance to living out the rest of her empty days in bitterness and asked that the women call her Mara ("bitter", v. 20). Ruth, on the other hand, moves on in faith (v. 16). It is significant that it is Ruth who holds the fresh barley stalks. She embodies the real spirit of the feast, even though the text does not mention the feast. Besides the literary connections with the previous context and the overlapping images and motifs, the structure of Ruth 1:1–7 highlights the transitional element: the "return" motif context of verse 1. Elimelech with his family left for Moab, which matches verses 6–7. Naomi set out to "return" because YHWH had provided food. Repetition of "return" in verses 6–7 strengthens the "return" motif in the second (1:7b–19a) and third scenes (1:19b–22a). Narrative constructions frame that "return" motif: and they went on their way to "return" to the land of Judah (v. 7b), so they both went on until they came to Bethlehem (v.19a).

The text includes several other references to the "return" theme, all in balanced relationships. Naomi's speech in verse 8, "Go, return each of you to your mother's house," balances her admonition to Ruth in verse 15b, "return after your sister-in-law." At the centre of this scene (vv. 10–13), the dialogue between Naomi, Ruth, and Orpah reflects the "return" motif. Moreover, they said to her: "we will surely return with you, to your people" (v. 10). Naomi said, "Return, my daughters … Return my daughters! Go for I am too old" (vv. 11–12).

The third scene continues to reinforce the "return" motif with another narrative bracket. Moreover, it came about when they had come to Bethlehem (v. 19). "So Naomi returned and with her Ruth the Moabite, her daughter-in-law, who returned from the land of Moab" (v. 22). When they came to Bethlehem, the whole town was stirred because of them; and the women said, "Is this Naomi?" (v. 19). It seems that after Naomi's arrival, the initial atmosphere was positive. However, Naomi quickly quashed that by saying, "call me Mara (bitter)."

Chapter 1 of Ruth is Earth-centred and Earth-dependent. These twenty-two verses depict how a flight from famine in Bethlehem to sustenance in Moab and a return to Earth's fruitfulness in Bethlehem prompts human actions.[3] However, Naomi does not recognize how central Earth and Earth's fruitfulness are to her existence. She defines "full" and "empty" in terms of male relatives. She left for Moab, not "full" but fleeing from famine, and she returned to Bethlehem, not "empty" but assured of Ruth's vow of loyalty to her, to her land and her god. Fortuitously Naomi and Ruth arrive in Bethlehem in time to benefit from the barley harvest.

Auspiciously, their arrival in Bethlehem coincides with the beginning of the barley harvest, a fruitful Earth welcome. Ruth 1:22 alerts us to the significance of

---

3. Pathos and irony pervade this chapter—despite Ruth's extraordinary vow of loyalty to Naomi and her God, and her choosing a future without promise or hope, Naomi ignores her as do the people of Bethlehem. The narrator calls her "Ruth the Moabite" (v. 22), even though it is with her that the future of Israel lies.

Earth's seasons and produce and highlights how Earth and Earth's activities lead
and drive the actions of the human characters in the Ruth narrative.

Chapter 2 begins with the narrator's reference to Boaz, a landowner and
Elimelech's relative. Ruth's request, "Let me go to the field and glean among the
ears of grain, behind someone in whose sight I may find favour," (2:2) highlights
her hope that the Earth of Judah will sustain Naomi and herself in their poverty.
She claims the right of the poor enshrined in the Law of Moses to glean at harvest
time. We read in Lev 19:9–10, "When you reap the harvest of your land, you shall
not reap to the very edges of your field, or gather the gleanings of your harvest.
You shall not strip your vineyard bare or gather the fallen grapes of your vineyard;
you shall leave them for the poor and the alien: I am the LORD your God." The
"field" is central to human actions throughout chapter 2. She came and gleaned
in the field behind the reapers. As it happened, she came to the part of the field
belonging to Boaz. The narrator attributes her arrival on Boaz's land to chance or
luck (*miqreh*).

The assumptions of a patriarchal society sound clearly in Boaz's question (2:5),
"to whom does this young woman belong?" as in the servant's response to Boaz's
question. He identifies Ruth not by name but as a Moabite and by her relationship
to Naomi. However, the servant also describes Ruth's unstinting labour, her
stamina, and perseverance, "without resting even for a moment" (*NRSV*) or "she
has been on her feet ever since she came this morning" (*JSB*); "she has hardly had
a moment's rest in the shelter." The workers, who also toil on the Earth, recognize
Ruth's closeness to Earth and her ability to "be on her feet" to be one with Earth
throughout the working day (2:7). Then Boaz said to Ruth, "Do not go to glean
in another field or leave this one but keep close to my young women" (2:8). "Keep
your eyes on the field they are reaping [being reaped] and follow behind them.
I have ordered the young men not to bother you." "If you get thirsty, go to the
vessels and drink from what the young men have drawn" (2:9).[4] At this point, Ruth
expresses her oneness with Earth, she falls prostrate, with her face to the ground/
Earth "*Eretz*" (2:10). At mealtime, Boaz tells her, "Come here, eat some bread,
and dip your morsel in the wine." He passed her parched grain, and she ate until
she was satisfied, and she had some left over. Boaz's offer of hospitality to Ruth
(2:14–16) also highlights the plentiful harvest and fruitful Earth. So, she gleaned
in the field until evening. Then she beat out what she had gleaned, and it was about
an ephah of barley (Ruth 2:13). Ruth knows how to obtain the best from her labour
in the field—she is one with the Earth (2:17–23).

4. Boaz's protection of Ruth (v. 9), "I have ordered the young men not to molest you"
contains echoes of the divine protection afforded to Sarah (Gen 20:6) and Rebecca (Gen
26:11). Ruth's response plays on the verb "acknowledge" and the noun foreigner (*nokri*), a
category of persons distinct from the "resident alien" (*ger*) who had legal rights of protection
within the community.

Barley and wheat harvests completed

Chapter 2:23 marks the end of the barley and wheat harvests and the beginning of a new uncertain future for the human characters, especially for those who must eke out a living by finding work on land owned by others. Widows and orphans were most at risk of gross neglect, so not surprisingly numerous Bible texts extol care for widows and orphans (Isa 1:17; Psa 68:5; Exod 22:21–24; Deut 27:19; Psa 146:9; Psa 82:3; Deut 10:18; Jer 49:11; Zach 10:7–10).

Naomi in 2:20 states an intriguing conviction in her prayer: "Blessed be he by the LORD, whose kindness has not forsaken the living or the dead." "The man is a relative of ours, one of our nearest kin." So while on the one hand, she offers thanks to the Lord, on the other, she claims that family/blood connections in the Earthly sphere are most effective. Was it luck that Ruth went to Boaz's field, rather than elsewhere (2:3)? By the end of the story, we see Naomi's prayer commending Ruth to God's hands fulfilled through the actions of the human characters, but it would not have happened if Ruth had not gone to the field of Boaz. Human action and divine action together lead to the survival of the community in Bethlehem that offers hope for recovery and fruitful harvests.

"Field" is pivotal in the narrative. Ruth and Boaz meet in a field, a fertile environment.[5] She comes from the "fields of Moab," and the mention of her Moabite origins reminds us that she is a foreign woman. She gleans in Boaz's field, then goes to the same field in chapter 3: Ruth; even though physically absent from the negotiations in 4:1–14, she is inseparable from the negotiations about the redemption of the field "parcel of land" belonging to Elimelech. The field is about to be sold or transferred to another owner by the "redeemer" *go'el*. Ruth is a field person, both in Moab and Judah. She travelled from the fields/land of Moab with Naomi, and on arriving in the land of Bethlehem goes by chance to the field of Boaz. Mention of Ruth's work in the field belonging to Boaz appears seven times in chapter 2—the eighth "field" allusion occurs in chapter 4 about another field, which is the field that belongs to Elimelech/Naomi and is under negotiation. Then, addressing the unnamed "*go'el*," Boaz said, "The day you acquire the field from the hand of Naomi, you are also acquiring Ruth the Moabite, the widow of the dead man, to maintain the dead man's name on his inheritance" (4:5).

In Ruth 3:1–14, the narrator highlights how the human characters depend totally on the Earth, and all its creatures. While Naomi takes the initiative[6] and the segment begins and ends with Ruth and Naomi in conversation, it centres on the crucial scene between Ruth and Boaz at the threshing floor. Ruth, as directed by Naomi, goes down to the threshing floor and lies on the Earth "at midnight—the man was startled and behold a woman lay at his feet" (Ruth 3:9). He said, "Who are you?" And she answered, "I am Ruth, your servant; spread your cloak over your

---

5. Amy-Jill Levine, "Ruth," in *Women's Bible Commentary*, ed. Carol A. Newsom and Sharon H. Ringe (Louisville, KY: Westminster John Knox, 1998).

6. Verse 20 claims that Boaz is a kinsman redeemer (*go'el*) (Lev 25:25, 47–49).

servant, for you are next-of-kin." Boaz calls Ruth "a valiant woman" or "woman of substance" *eshet hayil*.[7] Proverbs 31:10–31 portray the only other *eshet hayil* in the Hebrew Bible. Once more Earth provides as the darkness of night enables and witnesses the resolution of famine with the scene at the threshing floor amidst piles of harvested grain when a vulnerable foreign widow enters a dangerous place as a supplicant.

Emptiness and fullness

Themes of emptiness and fullness, prominent in Naomi's lament in 1:21, recur in 3:15–18. Ruth's gleanings of barley provide food for Naomi's physical emptiness and hunger and assuage her physical hunger. However, the grain crops are but a prelude to the satisfying of their more profound needs. Ruth's courageous entry to the threshing floor creates a tension in the narrative. Will she be rebuffed and driven away? Darkness shrouds her identity. Boaz on awakening must ask her to identify herself.

Ruth exits from the threshing floor also under cover of darkness. Verse 14 says, "She lay at his feet until dawn" but "she rose before one person could distinguish another" (or his friend), for Boaz said, "let it not be known that the woman came to the threshing floor." Darkness enables human actions to take place in secret, thus avoiding many problems. Decisions are dependent on night and day. The first light of day illumines Ruth's emergence with a further supply of grain and signals the treasure that Naomi will receive with Obed's birth and a promise of fulfilment. Naomi has the first and last word in chapter 3. Boaz's mention of a closer relative introduces an element of uncertainty into her carefully conceived plan. Once again, a hint of chance or luck comes into play. In 3:18, Naomi tells Ruth to wait and see how the matter will fall—no calling on God to intervene—the emphasis is on human action, patience, and loyalty—*hesed*.

Ruth 4:1–6 moves the action back to the public sphere and male participants exclusively as they engage in the apportioning of land rights and trade-offs for the marriage between Boaz and Ruth. Boaz plays his trump bargaining chip when he says to so and so—the man who would have the first right to the land under discussion. "The day you acquire the field from the hand of Naomi you are also acquiring Ruth the Moabite" (3:5,10). The marriage is apparently to maintain the dead man's name on his inheritance.

In Ruth 4:7–13, a group of elders (4:2) and the people (4:11) ratify the agreement concerning the property and the marriage. Significantly, the blessing in 4:1 compares Ruth to Rachel and Leah, mothers to the twelve sons of Jacob, the founding fathers of the twelve tribes (4:12). It also associates her with Tamar, who, like Ruth, was a foreigner. By unconventional means, Tamar secured the future of a line threatened by extinction (Gen 38). So, Ruth is not the first or sole foreign

---

7. The only other appearance of this term is in Proverbs 31:10 where it describes the *eshet hayil*.

woman named in the genealogy of the Davidic line. Divine intervention enables Ruth's conception of a son in 4:14–22. So, a story that began with Naomi, empty through famine and affliction, concludes with Ruth giving birth to a male child, Obed (4:15–17), who becomes Naomi's son and the grandfather of David. Thus, Naomi and Ruth achieve fullness—material security and a place in the genealogy of the Davidic line.

A final dual paradox appears. One leg supports a narrative that builds towards the significance of a male redeemer and a male heir. However, the praise of the women in Bethlehem in 4:15, "He shall be to you a restorer of life and a nourisher of your old age; for your daughter-in-law who loves you, who is more to you than seven sons, has borne him," suggests how the narrator evaluates the relative importance of males and females for Naomi. The women of the neighbourhood gave him a name, saying, "A son has been born to Naomi." They named him Obed; he became the father of Jesse, the father of David (4:18–23). Ridiculously, no female ancestors appear! However, the naming of the scroll is the final punchline—the book bears Ruth's name.

From a tale of famine, exile, death, and loss, the genealogy points to a glorious future in the reign of David. The canonical placement of Ruth in the Bible gives the story a broader significance than the purely domestic and introduces the promise of hope after the emptiness and despair with which the book of Judges ends. The narrator embodies in the experience of each of the human characters a contrast between death and life and offers examples of what it means to "choose life" as enjoined by Deut 30:11–20.

The flourishing or decline of Earth and the Earth community highlights the absolute dependence of human creatures on Earth and all its elements. Many interpreters regard Ruth as a simple village story, not a universal narrative. They envision the account as an ideal on a manageable scale that they can closely relate to their circumstances. In such interpretations, the narrative remains on a recognizably human plane with readers referring to the flesh-and-blood characters and to the picture of a social community that is far from ideal. By seeking to read Ruth from an Earth perspective and listen to Earth's voice in the narrative, we may recognize the story's embodiment of a this-worldly hope sustained by a narrator who invites the audience to identify with Earth and Earth's creatures in a struggle for survival. While the geographic locale and genealogy ultimately relate to David, the explicit focus of the narrative is concerned with Earth's actions rather than with divine activities.

Ruth and Naomi's courageous decisions suggest their attention to the voice of Earth and Earth's gifts as they bring to fruition Earth's blessings in this narrative. Such an emphasis demands recognition of social aspects of the action, especially how these enduring female characters escape poverty and starvation and wrest a modicum of security and the beginnings of a less precarious life from the Earth. Although women and men appear to work together at the end of the story, women must still wring concessions and opportunities out of the dominant male, patriarchal setting in which they live. An Earth reading of Ruth focuses on the actions of Earth and Earth's elements such as famine, exile, death, barley and wheat harvests, land ownership, and day and night, in contrast to concentrating on the contributions of the Deity to the favourable resolution of the story. Perhaps this reading brings a different perspective and theological weight to the concluding vision of survival and fullness.

Controversial aspects of some anthropocentric readings of Ruth tend to concentrate on the human figures as central to the narrative. Ruth interpretations laud Ruth's implicit self-sacrifice and highlight Naomi and Ruth's power to reap fullness and human liberation. An Earth reading compels readers to engage with how the characters work to get the best that their Earth situation makes available, and in Ruth's case she takes huge risks with little guarantee that the result may be the most desirable. Ruth's marriage to Boaz and the guarantee of inclusion of Naomi in the arrangements suggests that such economic security may be disguising female economic dependence. It seems clear that none of the characters genuinely escape the patriarchal system that is integral to the narrative in its time and place.

Nonetheless, the narrator does portray the practice of *hesed*, the presence of God, however compromised by mixed and complicated motives, and complex relationships, in the struggle for survival. Keeping in mind that Earth and Earth's surviving characters are engaged in a post-famine recovery effort, mixed motives and multifaceted relationships are at the heart of this struggle. Human relationships that work towards long-term survival demand physical endurance, adaptability to unpredictable weather patterns, and water and land scarcity or even failure. They must seek stability, economic security, and strategies for resolving conflicts over scarce resources. Further discussion of how this situation is resolved appears in chapter 6.

Ruth is a narrative in which Earth, Earth characters, and human actors are involved and resist consideration under a single viewpoint of an omniscient narrator. Sometimes women's contemporary concerns for freedom from patriarchy challenge and subvert any reading that praises women's altruism in the service of values such as the importance of preserving the male family line culturally presumed to be masculine.

The continuing struggle to find a way through this apparent hermeneutical impasse has marked the research of many feminist scholars, not only regarding this text but also, in principle, regarding scripture generally.[8] As feminist scholars correctly note, most Bible texts are in some way products of patriarchal cultures. The term "patriarchal" here does not refer solely to male–female relationships but includes the intricacy of intermingling hierarchies of race, class, religion, ethnicity, and so forth, to describe complex patterns of domination. From an ecological perspective, the resolution of the story of the Ruth narrative leaves many disturbing questions.

---

8. Katharine D. Sakenfeld, *Ruth: A Bible Commentary for Teaching and Preaching*, Interpretation (Louisville, KY: John Knox Press, 1999).

The first of these questions hinges on how the narrative appears to laud a societal structure, which links women's economic security to marriage, preferably to a rich man. A second issue arises from the assumption that it is necessary for men to exercise greater power or control than women in some situations. Do our cultures generally assign to men greater authority than they do to women? It is tempting to conclude that oppressive characteristics of the Ruth narrative easily compare with contemporary cultures. From an ecological perspective, the standard Hebrew Bible text of Ruth does assume male dominance and female subservience. If the Ruth story embodies values I do not share, how am I to give authority to it? Might there be some fruitful hermeneutical possibility in working with what the Ruth text offers in its images of Earth and Earth's creatures? We might do this by withdrawing from piecemeal and fractional criticisms of sections of the narrative that lead potentially to a rejection of every viewpoint suggested in the text. Many commentators centre their attention on the devotion of Ruth to Naomi, assuming the younger woman's altruistic concern for her mother-in-law. Reactions to this devotion vary.

A group of older, married women engaged in regular Bible study uniformly praised Ruth as an ideal daughter-in-law. On the other hand, a group of young, unmarried, professional women expressed severe anxiety that their future mothers-in-law and their churches would hold before them the story of Ruth. They sensed that the traditional family values of some cultures matched closely those they perceived in the text. In the face of concern for how they would relate to such expectations, most members of the group regarded the example of Ruth as a woman who chose an unconventional route for her life as being of little importance.

Likewise, the character of the relationship between the two women, especially the care of the younger woman for the older, was a central component in most appropriations of the story, particularly in traditional faith contexts. Throughout such discussions, it becomes clear that many church communities, especially where male preachers and pastors work, use this story to urge upon women a traditional role in families, a role of servant to mother-in-law and husband that might even precludes work outside the home. So, for much younger Christian women, Ruth can be an oppressive text.

The theme of women bound by economic structures is significant for some but does not arise for others. Reactions range from mystification to dismissal, to completely unimportant or to the enthusiastic endorsement of this angle for viewing the story. Some women justify decisions to work abroad by invoking the example of Ruth, who left her home country for a foreign land, made contacts, entered dangerous spaces, and succeeded in winning a rich husband who supported not only herself but also her mother-in-law. They claim and many believe that God will take care of them, just as God took care of Ruth. Some might question that Ruth's expression of loyalty to Naomi in 1:16–17 did not reveal compelling personal reasons for leaving Moab. It is important to remember that Ruth has already married a foreigner, so her second marriage to a foreigner is not unique for her! In assessing the book of Ruth from an ecological perspective, some attention is given to the male-centred legal proceedings at the gate and the male-focused blessing addressed to Boaz. Some readers find a hopeful counterpoint in the women-centred closing scene in chapter 4. It may be possible to accept the importance of a male heir and the conventional economic arrangements of financial support through a wealthy husband as a satisfactory social structure. Likewise, the human resolution of Naomi's loss, in which the women of Bethlehem say, "A son has been born to Naomi" (4:17), highlights the unclear inheritance structures suggested in the Ruth narrative. Inheritance patterns may be of some concern. Worries about the role of daughters-in-law may extend far beyond questions of working outside the home. What many might regard as the joyful climax of the book can be abhorrent for some women. Some teachers and preachers have used the text of Ruth to reinforce traditional relationships and patterns of family structures in local cultures. Coupled with this has been the use of the Ruth text to reinforce traditional patterns of economic dependence in marriage and an effort to replicate parts of the picture provided by the text without giving careful attention to the goal of the entire text.

In reading from an Earth perspective, readers discover that the Ruth story portrays a human community characterized by reciprocal relationships with Earth and Earth's elements. Human inhabitants of Earth communities are aware of their total dependence on Earth, Earth's produce, physical sustenance, weather, light, darkness, and all of Earth's creatures. They become aware that their survival may depend on the inclusion of all community members and outsiders such as migrants, foreigners, and those who once may have been enemies. These features, rather than their specific cultural expression or the precise means of achieving these ends within the story, portray how Earth and Earth elements and creatures are central to the Ruth narrative.

Many have emphasized that biblical language about God is metaphorical. This fundamental starting point for appropriating God language has consequences for our interpretation of texts from an Earth perspective. Does this text image political structures that are inadequate and offensive to liberationist and feminist readings? Some have reinterpreted the text by stating its underlying themes in fresh imagery that still embodies the original understanding. An Earth reading of Ruth points to an extended metaphor for God's creation, where God continues to renew the face of the Earth. Ruth presents a vision of hope that is microcosmic and in which Earth and Earth elements, such as crop failure or success, climate and weather vagaries, that severely affect land and crop fertility are part of the narrative. Food and work availability and many other Earth products play critical roles. Revisiting each of these distinctions is essential. The fundamental features described above are sustenance, inclusiveness, justice, and care for all. The particularity of the microcosmic image may lead some ecological scholars to see various culturally specific inadequacies of the vision. Our critical hindsight should warn us against placing too much value on our restatements of the concrete social structures that we suppose might adequately describe God's vision for the future. While it may be appropriate to question practices of other cultures past or present as failing to embody ecological concerns, we must avoid making absolute our ways of concretizing our Earth readings of this text.

The story of Ruth could not exist without human participants in the sense that the actions of the characters, most notably Ruth and Boaz, but also Naomi and the other men and women of the village, provide engaging characters that move the action along. In an ecological reading, the focus not only encompasses the notion of God working through Earth and all Earth creatures including the human characters but also highlights how all participate in God's work. Because of the traditionally anthropocentric bias of texts and interpreters' tendency to read from an anthropocentric viewpoint, it takes considerable effort to get to a view of the text where Earth and Earth elements are central and pivotal. Once the opening verses establish the disastrous situation of famine, flight, and death, the remainder of the story highlights just two direct interventions of God towards the restoration of wholeness and community.

God provides food in formerly famine-stricken Bethlehem (1:6), thus initiating the restoration, and God enables the conception of Obed by Ruth (4:13), thus bringing the restoration to fruition. These two divine acts may represent those aspects of the natural order over which ancient peoples experienced the least control. Elsewhere in Ruth, human beings call on God to do what they believe themselves unable to accomplish, as we see in Naomi's prayer in Ruth 1:8, "May YHWH deal with you kindly as you have dealt with the dead." Therefore, is the narrator showing God at work behind the human actions all of which are inseparable from Earth's ongoing momentum as experienced in famine and a plentiful harvest or its failure, fertility or infertility, life or death? Naomi states an intriguing conviction in her prayer in Ruth 2:20: "Blessed be he by YHWH whose kindness has not forsaken the living or the dead—the man is a relative of ours, one of our nearest kin."

So, while, on the one hand, she offers thanks to YHWH, on the other she claims family/blood connections in the Earthly sphere. Conspicuous in the story of Ruth is the power of famine and death and the evil of ethnic prejudice as obstacles the characters must overcome. Ruth begins, "In the days of the Judges there was a famine in the land." This era we know from the preceding book of Judges as one filled not just with Israelite warfare against external enemies but also with the most horrific internal struggles, murders, destruction, and devastation in which women are especially victimized (Judg 19–21). Over against such communal collapse, Ruth offers a narrative for a different way, initiated through an unexpected human source—a woman, a poor widow, an outsider from a despised group.

Chapter 3

RUTH: A FEMALE LIBERATOR

One of the major themes running through the book of Ruth highlights relationships of the human characters with Earth and all the elements of Earth. Underpinning this theme of relationship is an assumption about the weakness of women and the assumption that women could not own, buy, or sell land. Such an assumption clashes with Ruth chapter 4:3 that introduces Boaz as he is speaking to the closer next-of-kin, "Naomi, who has come back from the country of Moab, is selling the parcel of land that belonged to our kinsman Elimelech." Such a claim challenges a widely held belief that there was a lack of land for females.

In the story of Ruth, the culturally perceived "weakness" of women becomes a symbol for new concepts of power. I am assuming that after the return to the land from the Babylonian exile (538 BCE) life was exceedingly difficult politically and religiously. There may have been issues about returning Israelites who had lived outside Palestine. Returnees from the Babylonian exile conflicted with the people who had stayed in Palestine and with those who had moved on to the land after its devastation in 586 BCE. There were issues about leadership among the returnees to the land, and relationships with other foreign peoples and their gods rarely went harmoniously. Who was YHWH compared to Marduk or, later under the Greeks, compared to Zeus?

The book of Ruth in common with the books of Judith and Esther portrays its leading female characters as saviour figures. It appears likely that the book of Ruth was part of the significant literary and theological developments in the late post-exilic period (about 400–100 BCE). It probably was part of the evolution of the short story literary genre in the Bible. The Ruth narrative focuses on female characters as saviours of Israel. Ruth, Esther, and Judith are examples of this new literary type. Each of these stories follows a small group of characters through single brief plots to their resolutions.

The positioning of the book of Ruth in the Bible suggests a level of disagreement about its purpose in both Jewish and Christian traditions. We find similar stories in Gen 24, 38, 37, 39–50; 2 Sam 9–20; and 1 Kgs 1–2. However, these stories appear woven into larger books (scrolls), while Ruth, Judith, and Esther are free-standing books (scrolls). Ruth contains an episode from the period of the Judges, so in the Septuagint, this story appears after the book of Judges. Catholic and Protestant canons follow this order. The Hebrew canon places Ruth in the *Ketuvim*, the Writings. It stands next after the Song of Solomon, being the second of the Five Megillot.[1]

The Hebrew Bible/OT has several other vital women characters, for example, Deborah, Miriam, Huldah, and Bathsheba, but never had women played such a central role throughout an entire narrative. Furthermore, in these three books, women become liberators precisely because men failed to lead. The primary weapon of the principal women characters in these three narratives is their female sexuality: Ruth, Esther, and Judith highlight the contrast between male and female in the narrative. Judith exhibits military prowess, while Esther displays regal control, and Ruth demonstrates economic and social influence.

Female sexuality

Men cannot provide for the people, so Judith, a beautiful widow, Esther, a comely and assertive queen, and Ruth, a sexually aggressive foreigner, succeed in achieving success in each case. A foreigner, an orphan, and a widow are stereotypes of weakness in a world dominated by males. These three female characters by beauty, cunningness, and assertiveness save both themselves and the Jewish people, Judith and Ruth in Israel and Esther in the Diaspora. Are these three books stories for the weak post-exilic communities that live in hostile environments? The earlier reliance on military prowess and the Davidic dynasty had failed the nation. The survivor communities must now look for strength within their apparent weaknesses.

Stories of liberation

Each of these stories has a unique concept of liberation. Each of the main female characters frees her people from oppression. As a foreigner and a childless widow, Ruth was dependent on the beneficence of others for her survival. The attitude of the narrator in the book of Ruth towards non-Jews is surprising, as there seems to be little animosity or discrimination towards Ruth as a Moabite other than to identify her as a foreign widow. While many other Bible texts refer disparagingly to Moab and Moabites, no such allusions appear in the Ruth text.

Ruth brings about the resolution of famine on a threshing floor amid quantities of harvested grain. She, a vulnerable woman, enters a dangerous setting as a supplicant and emerges with a guarantee of marriage and with the immediate reward of grain to take back to her household. She now has control of her future and consequently of Naomi's future also. The author chose the barley field and later

---

1. Observant Jews read the book of Ruth on *Shavuot*, the festival celebrating the giving of the Torah to the Israelites.

the threshing floor as the settings where Ruth disempowers the powerful Boaz. Thus, the narrative portrays how the settings in which she appears empower Ruth, the so-called weak, to triumph over all her perceived obstacles. In the scene at the threshing floor, the irony appears in the comparison implied by Boaz's blessing.

There is a marked development in how Ruth is described—for example, Ruth calls herself by different names in 2:10, 2:13, and 3:9; others address Ruth differently in 2:5, 2:8, 3:11, and 4:11. But progression in naming Ruth marks developments in the narrative.

I now move from literary considerations of the book of Ruth to the theology that the literary features expressed in the narrative. I see the book of Ruth as falling into five major sections. The first of these covers the famine and the ensuing flight of Elimelech, Naomi, Chilion, and Mahlon from Bethlehem to Moab, the ten-year sojourn in Moab, Naomi's decision to return to Bethlehem, and Ruth's decision to accompany Naomi. Thus, Ruth, a Moabite widow, now becomes an exile in Bethlehem. The genealogy in the book of Ruth portrays her as the grandmother of King David, and the Gospel of Matthew names her as an ancestor of the Messiah. Flanking the upper corners of the painting are birds holding in their beaks the names of Ruth and Naomi, probably suggested by *Te Talmud Ruth* that refers to Ruth as a beautiful bird of love and kindness that flew over from the Moabites.

Transitions in Ruth

This story hinges on several connecting scenes. The narrator takes up features in Ruth 1:1–22 and resolves them in Ruth 4:13–22. A series of transitions throughout the narrative characterize the narrative. Such connections mark the transition from the scene they complete to the scene that follows as illustrated in 1:22 that is the first of these. This verse moves the setting from Naomi and Ruth's journey from Moab to the scene where the two widows embark on finding sustenance in the land of Israel. Ruth decides to go out to glean in the barley harvest. By a lucky chance, she goes to a field that belongs to Boaz, who is Naomi's relative. This scene concludes at 2:23, where Naomi instructs Ruth about the strategy of going to the threshing floor at night and engaging with Boaz there under cover of darkness.

The transition and connection here are in 3:18, where Ruth leaves Boaz at the threshing floor before anyone could recognize her and returns to Naomi with an account of how her strategy had succeeded. Boaz becomes the central character in the next scene as he sets about becoming Ruth and Naomi's *gōĕl* by negotiating the sale of the field that belongs to Naomi and arranging his marriage to Ruth. To achieve this goal, he must first ensure that a closer relative must either become the *gōĕl* or opt out of the obligation. This Boaz arranges by organizing a meeting of the elders at the city gate. It seems his main aim is to manage the situation to the advantage of the needy! The transition occurs here in 4:13 at the city gate and concludes with the birth of the child.

Symmetry

Examples of symmetry also mark the Ruth narrative. Ruth 1:1 says that Elimelech, Naomi, and their sons Mahlon and Chilion flee famine in Bethlehem and journey to Moab in search of food. This journey results in a ten-year stay in Moab, where the narrator text tells of death and sterility. Elimelech dies, leaving Naomi a widow. The two sons, Mahlon and Chilion, marry Moabite women Ruth and Orpah, but the two "boys" die, leaving both women widows. This brief account of the death of husbands and the plight of the three widows contrasts sharply with chapter 4 where Boaz "redeems the field that belongs to Naomi, Ruth and Boaz marry; conceive a child, and Ruth gives birth to a boy, Obed, who will be the grandfather of King David."

Ruth chapters 2–3 reveal similarities; for example, Ruth and Naomi decide on a strategy to obtain food in order to survive. Ruth goes to glean in the barley field that, by chance, belongs to Boaz. When Boaz arrives at the field, he asks who she is and learns from one of his servants that she is the Moabite widow who has come from Moab. She has been kind to her mother-in-law Naomi and has been working all day, not even taking time to rest in the shelter. Boaz invites her to drink the water provided by the servants. He provides her with food and drink at mealtime. She even has some food leftover to take back to Naomi who may have been dependant on what Ruth could bring back from her day's gleaning. In scene 3, Ruth and Naomi plot their next survival strategy. Once more, Ruth will undertake this endeavour. Naomi tells Ruth to dress up, anoint herself, and go down to the threshing floor at night where she will encounter Boaz.

Boaz's place in the plot

Interestingly, Boaz and Naomi never meet in the narrative. She claims him as a relative, yet all their engagement is at second or third hand. This distancing of two central characters seriously enhances Ruth's role in the story. Boaz is a figure who is vital to the plot as he is necessary for the preservation of Ruth and Naomi, yet the narrator makes it clear in several ways that Boaz is primarily a tool used and manipulated by the women, with very little value of his own aside from his role as redeemer. While Boaz appears to be central, a vital member of the cast and the only principal male, yet the narrator portrays him as a marginalized character by pushing him to the edges. His actions are reactions. While his function in the plot is necessary, yet it is contingent upon the two women around whom this story revolves.

Many scholars have divided the four chapters of the book of Ruth into four scenes with actions attributed to different characters in each. In chapter 1, Naomi is the primary mover as she decides to return to Bethlehem and sets off the chain of events about which the book is concerned. Ruth becomes the active agent in chapter 2 as she takes charge of their desperate situation and sets out to provide sustenance. Most readers see chapter 3 as belonging to Naomi, for although Ruth is the one who must go to the threshing floor under cover of darkness to meet Boaz; Naomi lays out the plan for her daughter-in-law. Finally, in chapter 4, the action undoubtedly belongs to Boaz.

While the narrator mentions Elimelech before Naomi in the opening verses of the story, by the third verse, he becomes the husband of Naomi. The narrative implies that the husband decided to leave Bethlehem and go to the fields of Moab, yet neither he nor his sons ever speak. The primary function of Elimelech and his sons is to die and thus bring about the crisis upon which the story turns. It is at the point when the three husbands are dead that the story begins, and Naomi becomes the subject. "Then she started to return with her daughters-in-law from the country of Moab." It is Naomi, by her decision to return to Judah, and her urging of her daughters-in-law to remain in Moab "to return to your mother's house," who prompts Ruth to leave her own home and gods and to go to Bethlehem with her mother-in-law.[2] Chapter 1 focuses readers' attention on the plight of these women, themselves representing two of the most vulnerable classes of people, both are widows, and one is a foreigner, a Moabite. The men who were the driving force in the opening two verses of the narrative are all dead by 1:5. As Phyllis Trible so succinctly notes, "The males die; they are nonpersons; their presence in the story ceases … The females live; they are persons; their presence in the story continues. Indeed their life is the life of the story."[3]

Chapter 1 concludes with Ruth's declaration of loyalty to Naomi. Ruth's unequivocal statement to her mother-in-law is that she will remain with Naomi until death. Linafelt notes that the speech used by Ruth and Naomi is in the form of poetry, setting their words aside from the rest of the narrative and bringing the first chapter to a conclusion with a clear focus on the two women as the central characters of the story. By contrast, Boaz "is confirmed in this reading as secondary to these two women."[4] The chapter concludes with the two women headed for Bethlehem "at the beginning of the barley harvest" (1:22). God has lifted the famine from the land, but it has fallen upon Naomi and her daughter-in-law, who is a "Moabite."

In chapter 2, Boaz appears in the barley field. Readers are aware of his existence before Ruth knows of his existence. In chapter 1, Naomi encouraged her daughters-in-law to return to their mother's house in the hope that they would "find security … in the house of your husband" (Ruth 1:9) but she never speaks of finding a husband for herself. She does not appear to consider the possibility of a male redeemer, or if she does, she does not express this hope. The narrator mentions

---

2. Ruth is the *primary* mover in the narrative. She insists to Naomi that she returns with her, and it is she who drives the story onwards.

3. Phyllis Trible, *God and the Rhetoric of Sexuality* (Philadelphia, PA: Fortress Press, 1987), 168–9.

4. Tod Linafelt and Timothy K. Beal, *Ruth and Esther*, Berit Olam (Collegeville, PA: Liturgical Press, 1999).

Boaz to prepare the audience for his entrance.[5] He steps into view only after Ruth has taken the initiative and has gone to glean to find food for herself and Naomi.

The narrator introduces Boaz by telling his audience that he is a great man.[6] Whether this means he is powerful or wealthy or both, we never learn. "Naomi had a relative of her husband's, a man of wealth/substance; of the family of Elimelech whose name was Boaz." Interestingly, this wealthy man only reacts to Ruth's initiative; her presence prompts him to inquire about her. His speech to Ruth makes it clear that he knew of Naomi's return from Moab and of Ruth's decision to accompany her mother-in-law to Bethlehem. "All you have done for your mother-in-law since the death of your husband has been fully told me." Campbell's observations on why Boaz is so tardy in getting in touch with Naomi on her return are unconvincing. It is inherent in biblical thought generally that a persons' actions and words offer an accurate picture of the person's character.

In the case of Boaz, what we find is what the character is. We could make up a backstory as the rabbinic sources have done and provided him with motives for not engaging with Naomi and Ruth before this event in the field. On the other hand, we could accept that Boaz does not enter the story proper up to this point because the author intended it to be this way; he had no use for Boaz until this time in the story. His character is marginal, he only makes an appearance when necessary, and he does not initiate anything but instead reacts to Ruth's decisions and actions. The fact that Boaz remains in reserve and is more reactive than proactive does not mean that his character is without qualities that we can discern from the text. When he arrives at his field, he greets his workers with the name of God. "The Lord is with you" is the first of two blessings that Boaz offers in this chapter in the name of God (2:4 and 2:12).

Most modern commentators understand the initial greeting to the workers as a simple, conventional greeting.[7] Linafelt's suggestion that Campbell and Nielsen's view of this greeting as "an indication of Boaz's great piety or moral character seems to overstate the case."[8] What commentators have done is consider the initial, customary greeting in combination with Boaz's blessing of Ruth. These invocations of the name of God may be an original from Boaz to God in light of Ruth's

5. Bush notes that Boaz's identity is given in relation to Naomi: "Naomi had a kinsman on her husband's side" (Bush 49).

6. See Anthony Hubbard, *The Book of Ruth*, NICOT (Grand Rapids, MI: Eerdmans), 90. The term is much debated and variously translated: "a mighty man of wealth" in the KJV, "a prominent rich man" in the NRSV, "a man of substance" in JPS, and "a man of standing" in the NIV. As Hubbard points out, "The translation 'man of substance' has just the right ambiguity to cover the term in Hebrew."

7. See, for example, Hubbard, *The Book of Ruth*, 144, particularly notes 14 and 15; Kirsten Nielsen, *Ruth: A Commentary*, trans., Edward Broadbridge, OTL (Louisville, KY: Westminster John Knox), 57. Edward F. Campbell, *Ruth. AB 7* (New York: Doubleday, 1975), 112.

8. Linafelt and Beal, *Ruth & Esther*, 29.

faithfulness to Naomi.[9] So an image of Boaz emerges as of a man who, in words at least, views the Lord as central to the blessing and survival of his people. We cannot speak of Boaz's devotion beyond this since the narrator does not provide us with additional insights into what today we might call his theological convictions. We should, however, consider his actions even as he considers and praises Ruth's actions towards her mother-in-law. Once the narrator has introduced Boaz into the narrative, and he becomes aware of Ruth, he immediately begins to take steps that will ensure her and Naomi's well-being.

Linafelt makes an important point when he notes how Ruth questions Boaz as to why he should treat her so well (2:10). "Her question may be an expression of gratitude but is also a genuine question. Ruth is probing his motivations for showing her 'favour' and for singling her out for attention."[10] However, Linafelt is not satisfied with Boaz's response and reads his invocation of the Lord as an effort to deflect his real interest, which is Ruth. While there is some inherent sexual tension here, nothing in the text suggests that his initial actions are anything other than a response to her *hesed* towards Naomi. However, his behaviour may indicate his interest in Ruth. He calls Ruth over to him at mealtime and even prepares her food (Ruth 2:14), and even directs his servants to ensure that she gets plenty of grain stalks by allowing her to glean far beyond what the law stipulates.

By the time she returns to Naomi, Ruth has a sense of who Boaz is and that he has shown some interest in her. What she does not appear to know yet but which the audience does know is that he is Naomi's relative and is a wealthy man. In the field, he demonstrates that his custom and worldview include invoking the name of the Lord and that he blesses those who show *hesed* to others. He shows *hesed* to Ruth when he ensures her safety in the barley field and provides favourable conditions for her while she gleans for barley for herself and Naomi. Considering the text thus far, the narrator does not highlight Boaz as a man of great piety and devotion; it does seem that at this point in the story the narrator presents Boaz as a good man.[11]

Many view chapter 3 as Naomi's since it opens with Naomi taking responsibility for Ruth's well-being: "I need to seek some security for you so that it may be well with you" (3:1). Naomi also cooks up a plan for Ruth to present herself to Boaz at night on the threshing floor. On the other hand, it is Ruth who not only acts out that plan but also goes beyond Naomi's instructions.[12] The opening verse of chapter 3 indicates that readers' attention should now focus on Ruth rather than on Boaz. Whether readers consider Naomi or Ruth the primary mover in

---

9. "May the LORD reward you for your deeds, and may you have a full reward from the LORD, the God of Israel, under whose wings you have come for refuge" (Ruth 2:12).

10. Linafelt and Beal, *Ruth & Esther*, 36.

11. See, for example, André LaCocque, *Ruth: A Continental Commentary*, trans. H. C. Hanson (Minneapolis, MN: Fortress), 65.

12. In Ruth 3:4, Naomi says, "Go and uncover [Boaz's] feet and lie down; and he will tell you what to do." When the time comes Ruth, in fact, tells Boaz what to do.

chapter 3, the narrator leaves Boaz to react to the decisions made by the two female characters. When Boaz awakes on the threshing floor and realizes that he has an intruder, Ruth identifies herself and rather than waiting for directions or reactions tells him directly what he is to do. "I am Ruth, your servant; spread your cloak over your servant, for you are next of kin" (Ruth 3:9). Once again, while readers speculate about what Boaz might have said if Ruth had not directed him, the narrator provides Boaz's words. He invokes the Lord's blessing on Ruth because of her *ḥesed*.[13] While some judge Boaz's blessing to be feigned piety, others accept this as a positive aspect of Boaz character. He is a complex figure with good intentions and a firm grasp of the dangerous social situation confronting him. His speedy recovery suggests that he is accustomed to being in the lead position.

The fact that Boaz seems to affirm Ruth's request for marriage has struck some as odd. "This last instance of your loyalty is better than your first; you have not gone after young men, whether poor or rich" (3:10). However, while the question of whether or not the marriage between Boaz and Ruth is a levirate marriage is beyond the scope of this chapter, it does influence how one perceives this text and Boaz's response to Ruth's request. The problem is a difficult one but given the way the story progresses in chapter 4, it seems reasonable to conclude with Campbell that Ruth's presupposition that the responsibilities of redemption and marriage belong together seems compelling as the story progresses.

Most scholars concur in arguing that the final chapter is Boaz's since it is primarily concerned with his actions at the city gate, his "taking" Ruth as his wife, and the subsequent conception and birth of Obed. The activity of chapter 4, as many have noted, takes place in a male world.[14] The actions all move quickly and succinctly. Boaz has taken charge, and as Naomi had assured Ruth, he did not rest until he had settled the matter. Scholars continue to debate the details and historicity of the events described in chapter 4. Campbell urges interpreters to "approach the scene with the expectation that things should make sense, despite the ocean of ink which has been spilt over several unanswered questions raised by the scene."[15] While chapter 4 raises several issues, the immediate issue is the character of Boaz.

Chapter 4 opens with the first few words announcing that Boaz has arrived at the city gate and already begun conferring with "So and So" (Hebrew) regarding the parcel of land belonging to Elimelech and now for sale on behalf of Naomi. Then after some formalities and blessings, "Boaz took Ruth, and she became his wife" (4:12). The events move swiftly, and Boaz deftly manoeuvres the negotiations

---

13. While there is disagreement as to what, if any, is the single theme of Ruth (see Hubbard, *The Book of Ruth*, 35ff.), almost all commentators, ancient and modern, rightly note that *ḥesed* is a strong theme of the book of Ruth. See, for example, Campbell, 29–30; Nielsen, *Ruth*, 31.

14. "This public gathering is entirely a man's world, Trible notes that it is in scene four that 'Boaz takes charge.'"

15. Campbell, 154.

so that they reach a satisfactory conclusion in his and Ruth's favour. He has done all that he has promised to Ruth, and the result is marriage, offspring, and the perpetuation of the names of the deceased and of course the assurance of the ultimate birth of King David, great grandson of Obed Ruth's son.

All these proceedings occur in the realm of men. There are no women among the elders, and neither Ruth nor Naomi speaks again in the story. The only women who speak are the women of the community (Ruth 4:14–15, 17).[16] These same women were so startled at the state of Naomi upon her return to Bethlehem from Moab that they exclaimed, "Is this Naomi?" Now they conclude the story of Naomi's restoration by declaring, "Blessed be the Lord, who has not left you this day without next-of-kin; and may his name be renowned in Israel!" After praising God, they remind Naomi and their audience that the agent of this deliverance was Ruth, "for your daughter-in-law, who loves you, who is more to you than seven sons, has borne him." Although the two main female characters are silent, the author appears to highlight the point that this is their story, and it has come about because they drove the plot. One interpretation of the pivotal scene at the city gate in 4:5 may be, "The day that you acquire the field from the hand of Naomi, I also acquire Ruth the Moabite … in order to restore the name of the dead to his inheritance." Here Boaz may be exploiting a legal loophole as the next of kin may acquire Naomi's, really Elimelech's field as *gōĕl* Redeemer—a fair profit since Naomi has no prospects of offspring to claim the field later.

Boaz then announces his Levirate marriage to Ruth in order to restore Naomi's dead offspring. If Boaz and Ruth have a child, they would have a right to reclaim the field from the *gōĕl* Redeemer. The *gōĕl* promptly loses interest. His decision may explain why Ruth's son Obed is in a sense Naomi's son (4:14). The swift and decisive action by Boaz at the city gate would not have occurred if Ruth had not confronted him with the demand: "Spread your cloak over your servant, for you are next of kin." Even when it seems that this fantastic story of women's initiative is challenged at the very end by the silencing of the main characters and Boaz's emergence onto centre stage, the primary mover of these events remains Ruth. Furthermore, the end of the story belongs to Naomi and Ruth as the women of the community step forward and bless Naomi and name the child, "A son has been borne to Naomi."[17] There is no doubt that Boaz is a crucial player in the book of Ruth. The narrator makes it clear that Boaz, the male *gōĕl*, ensures safety and security for Naomi and Ruth. At the same time, the narrative restricts Boaz's engagement to one of reacting to Ruth.

However, it is the women and specifically the foreign woman Ruth who directs and propels the decision making. As a character, Boaz has more in common with

16. It is possible, even likely, that women are also included in the statement of witnesses in Ruth 4:9 since the text specifies it is "the elders and *all the people*."

17. Phyllis Trible, "Ruth," in *ABD*, ed. D. N. Freedman (New York: Doubleday, 1992). "The women of Bethlehem do not permit this transformation to prevail. They reinterpret the language of a man's world to preserve the integrity of a woman's story."

Rachel and Leah than with Jacob. He has certain critical moments of dialogue that move the plot forward, but ultimately, his primary function is to provide security and offspring. Ruth exhibits several similarities to Gen 12. Abraham and Ruth leave their homelands and decide the land of Israel will be their burial place. Ruth 4:11–12 compares Ruth with Rachel, Leah, and Tamar in Gen 29, 30, and 38. Verses 18–22 provide the relevant genealogy that leads to King David: "Now these are the descendants of Perez … Salmon of Boaz, Boaz of Obed, Obed of Jesse, and Jesse of David. We hear a version of this genealogy in Matt 1:3-6: Judah the father of Perez and Zerah by Tamar, and Perez the father of Hezron … father of Salmon, and Salmon the father of Boaz by Rahab, and Boaz the father of Obed by Ruth, and Obed the father of Jesse, and Jesse the father of King David. Moreover, David was the father of Solomon by the wife of Uriah."

The book of Ruth describes two women urgently in need of food and shelter. The complete narrative works towards how Ruth and Naomi collude to bring about a resolution of their poverty. Naomi is the cunning character who thought of a way to help both Ruth and herself. She puts this plan forward to Ruth (3:1-5) as she needs her cooperation. The negotiations may be invoking two customs that of *gōĕl* Redeemer and of Levirate marriage, thus providing for both widows. Ruth at Naomi's behest and conniving undertakes to force Boaz to undertake his role of *gōĕl* Redeemer for both herself and Naomi. The arrangements in Ruth are unrivalled in the Hebrew Bible. This is a short story, not a law journal, so the author and narrator could dispense with legalities and interpret the action in ways favourable to a beneficent outcome for all the deserving characters.

Chapter 4

RUTH: A LANDLESS MOABITE

In the story of Ruth, the culturally perceived "weakness" of women becomes a symbol for new concepts of power. The centuries after the return from the Babylonian exile (538 BCE) were difficult politically and religiously. The glorious New Exodus promised by Isaiah 40–55, and the fulfilment of the threefold divine promise announced by the exilic priestly writer, seemed empty. Those returning from the Babylonian exile found themselves in direct conflict with most of the people who had stayed in Palestine after its devastation by Nebuchadnezzar in 586 BCE. The main issue was who would assume leadership of the community now that the Davidic Dynasty was no longer in power and the Temple of Solomon was in ruins. The Persian king Cyrus had given funds for its reconstruction. However, which line of the priesthood would assume control of the new shrine? Would it be the Levites, who were a Mosaic priesthood, or the Zadokites, who traced their lineage to David's appointee Zadok? Furthermore, supporters of the Davidic royal family hoped to restore a survivor of that dynasty to the throne. Persian rulers would have regarded efforts to restore the kingship as a rebellion and suppressed them. Compounding these destabilizing factors was the immediate problem of reconciling the diminished situation with the more grandiose theology of the monarchy. How could the people become accustomed to understanding the divine promises of a permanent dynasty in Jerusalem (Davidic Covenant) given the occupation of the Promised Land by a foreign power? How could they reconcile the exalted status of Mount Zion (Zion Tradition) with the perilous situation after 586 BCE?

The Israelites had to face the problem of their relationship with other peoples and other gods. Who was Yahweh compared to Marduk or, later under the Greeks, compared to Zeus? There was also the dilemma of Jews living outside of Palestine (the Diaspora). After 586 BCE, Jews had settled over the entire eastern Mediterranean in Asia Minor, Egypt, and Mesopotamia. How could they worship Yahweh in foreign lands? Under the Persians (about 540–330 BCE), the reforms of Ezra addressed much of this turmoil. These reforms resulted in the adoption of the Law (perhaps the Pentateuch). After Alexander the Great conquered the Persian Empire, a succession of Hellenistic states ruled this area. The amalgamation of Greek culture and Near Eastern features resulted in the uniquely cosmopolitan civilization called Hellenism. This culture proved particularly seductive to many

Jews. Many accommodated their religion to this new movement; others fiercely resisted its encroachments; nevertheless, almost all used its thoughts and language to express their belief in YHWH.

In the late post-exilic period (about 400–100 BCE), we encounter two significant developments, one literary and the other theological. The evolution of the literary genre of the short story in the Bible and a focus on women as saviours of Israel appear in Ruth, Esther, and Judith. These short stories exemplify this new literary form. Each of the stories follows a small group of characters through a single brief plot to its resolution. Other examples of similar stories are in Gen 24, 38; the Joseph saga in Gen 37, 39–50; and the Davidic succession story in 2 Sam 9–20 and 1 Kgs 1–2. However, these stories are interwoven into larger books (Scrolls), while Ruth, Judith, and Esther are free-standing books (scrolls). Although scholars continue to debate the dating of these works, many agree that they are later developments. The book of Ruth, which is poetically idyllic, although the narrative is in the form of prose, contains an episode from the period of the Judges.

Perhaps this is the reason why it appears in the Septuagint after the book of Judges. The Vulgate follows this order as do the Catholic and Protestant canons. The Hebrew Bible places Ruth in the "Ketuvim," or third part of the Hebrew canon called the Megillot—Song of Songs, Ruth, Lamentations, Ecclesiastes, and Esther. Ruth takes its name from Ruth, the main character, who, with her mother-in-law, Naomi, is its heroine. The story is as follows: Elimelech, a man of Bethlehem-Judah, with his wife, Naomi, and his two sons, Mahlon and Chilion, went in the time of famine and sojourned in the land of Moab. Elimelech, Naomi's husband, died. The two sons married Moabites—Mahlon married Ruth, and Chilion married Orpah. Later, Mahlon and Chilion died. Sometime later, Naomi heard that the famine in Judah had passed. She decided to return home to Bethlehem. Ruth, despite the dissuasion of Naomi, accompanied her mother-in-law to Bethlehem and cast in her lot with the people of Judah.

Naomi and Ruth arrived in Bethlehem at the beginning of the barley harvest. Naomi's husband Elimelech had had an inheritance of land among his people, but, unless the women could find a *gōĕl* Naomi would be compelled to sell it. Now Naomi had a kinsman on her husband's side, a prominent rich man of the family of Elimelech whose name was Boaz. Ruth the Moabite said to Naomi, "Let me go to the field and glean among the ears of grain, behind someone in whose sight I may find favour." She said to her, "Go, my daughter." So she went. She came and gleaned in the field behind the reapers. As it happened, she came to the part of the field belonging to Boaz who was of the family of Elimelech. Just then, Boaz came from Bethlehem (Ruth 2:1–4).

After he had spoken kindly to her and shown her some favours, she, still acting upon the advice of her mother-in-law, approached Boaz at night and put herself in his power. Boaz was attracted to her but informed her that there was a kinsman nearer than he who had the first right to redeem the estate of Elimelech and that it would be necessary for this kinsman to renounce his right before Boaz could proceed in the matter. Accordingly, Boaz called this kinsman to the city gate before the elders and told him of the condition of Naomi and Ruth and the kinsman's right to redeem Elimelech's land and to marry Ruth. The kinsman declared that he did not wish to do so and took off his shoe—by which he renounced his right to the land in favour of Boaz (Ruth 4:7–9). Then Boaz said to the elders and all the people, "Today you are witnesses that I have acquired from the hand of Naomi all that belonged to Elimelech and all that belonged to Chilion and Mahlon. I have also acquired Ruth the Moabite, the wife of Mahlon, to be my wife, to maintain the dead man's name on his inheritance, in order that the name of the dead may not be cut off from his kindred and from the gate of his native place; today you are witnesses." (Ruth 4:1 NRS)

The Hebrew Scriptures had already portrayed Deborah (Judg 4:4), Miriam (Exod 15:2), Huldah (2 Kgs 22:14), and Bathsheba (2 Sam 11:3), as significant women. Never had women played a central role throughout an entire plot. Furthermore, in Ruth, Esther, and Judith, women become liberators precisely because men have failed. These short stories emphasize contrasts between male and female behaviours. The principles of military prowess (book of Judith), regal control (book of Esther), and economic/social influence (book of Ruth) are incapable of providing for the Jews and are superseded by a beautiful widow (Judith), a gifted and assertive queen (Esther), and an attractive and dynamic foreigner (Ruth). In all three of these stories, the primary weapon of the woman is her female sexuality. All three female characters, a foreigner, an orphan, and a widow, are stereotypes of vulnerability in a world dominated by males. By their beauty, cunningness, and assertiveness, they save both themselves and the Jewish people, whether at home in Israel (Judith and Ruth) or in the Diaspora (Esther). These three books are ideal exemplars for the weak post-exilic Israelite community in hostile environments. The long-standing reliance on military prowess and the Davidic dynasty had failed the Israelites. These changes compelled people to look for strength within their weaknesses.

Because Judah and Israel were no longer independent states in control of their destinies, the believers found themselves either scattered throughout the eastern Mediterranean (the Diaspora) or clustered in small villages in Palestine vulnerable to the whims of distant rulers. In either case, Jews had to face the issue of their relationships with gentiles. At this point, we must form an idea about the different ways in which post-exilic Jews related to the Gentile world in which they were obliged to live.

In the book of Ruth, "food and banquets" appear at decisive moments in the story. The resolution of famine occurs on a threshing floor amidst piles of harvested grain. A vulnerable woman entered an intimidating scene as a supplicant but emerged in complete control. Interestingly, the author chooses this moment of plenty in order to pull down the mighty or the powerful and to raise the weak. These paired and repeated words give some clues to how God functions. In the above list, God is portrayed as accomplishing something or is asked in prayer to accomplish something. The irony here is that usually the suppliant has the means to carry out what he/she has prayed for. This pattern suggests that human beings in Ruth usually can find the means to bring to fruition what first appears impossible.

Many scholars now emphasize that the book of Ruth presents a different conception of the Torah. Elimelech's family radically distinguishes itself from other

Israelite families in that it initially looked for refuge in Moab for its subsistence and its perpetuation. This first movement in the book is essential, for it establishes the background on which the whole story is built right up to the conclusion. Difference marks the principal characters of the book. Ruth is a Moabite woman, but not like the rest of her people. She becomes Israel's blessing, while her ancestors had paid Balaam to curse Israel. Naomi is a widow and "bitter." Unlike many widows without children in Israel, she eventually receives loyalty, affection, succession, and generation. Boaz comes from Bethlehem, but he goes decidedly against the grain. More fundamentally, the difference in Ruth is a generous and expansive understanding of the Law.

Another question posed by the deconstructionist (postmodern) movement would concern what the structure of the book of Ruth excludes from its perspective. What does it suppress? The question is pertinent, but it is surprisingly minimized by the fact that Ruth is precisely a protest, a subversion of Israel's legal system. Excluded also is a kind of male fundamentalist patriarchalism and its paternalistic attitude, of which (the old) Boaz displayed an example in Ruth 2. Also missing is a narrow, complacent nationalism prone to create a spirit of harsh judgment on "the others," that is, the Moabites, the foreign women, the barren ones, and the "losers." However, all that the book of Ruth excludes is insignificant in comparison with what it includes. In the book, one voice nevertheless became inaudible, that of Orpah. Of course, the narrative did not stifle her, for she was able to express herself, and even, in all liberty, give a sudden change of direction to her speech (1:10, 15). However, once she made another choice, in contrast to her alter ego Ruth, she became "the hollowed side" of Ruth's speech. Orpah becomes what Ruth could have been and refused to be. If the author continued to give free expression to Orpah's speech, she would have maintained ambivalence that Ruth categorically refused (1:16).

Similarly, Boaz rejects the predictable narrowness personified in so and so's choice. It is therefore verified once again in the instance of the book of Ruth that indeed all construction—even irenic—does violence to what remains unexpressed. However, one must immediately add that Orpah is not an outcast or a scapegoat. She leaves and returns to her mother's house—her natural group as she has been invited to by Naomi/Israel to do. In this way, she returns to the ordinary, not the aberrant. Ruth, by contrast, chooses the extraordinary and the extravagant, and this is how her existential choice is immediately interpreted (1:15). After the Moabite prelude, the narrator transports readers to Bethlehem, where a new pair of differences are brought into play and become the reason for the story. The confrontation switches to the level of a literal interpretation of the Law—according to which the presence of Ruth in Bethlehem is unbearable, and an extensive reading that recognizes that the Law is less a dictation than an orientation. The faithful must continually reinterpret obedience to the Law. The critical term is *ḥesed* because the key to the Law is freely given love implying the refusal of "categorizing" others. Even the Moabite must be integrated—and more than integrated since she becomes the exemplary model of *ḥesed*, the very basis of God's covenant with God's people is in a way rewritten. The ancient rabbis saw this. They concluded from the story of Ruth that the legal ostracism imposed on the Moabites should be interpreted as affecting the men of these people, not their women. This rabbinic readjustment is again insufficient, but the move goes in the right direction. Ruth "rewrites" the Torah. According to this rewriting, Israel's election is inclusive. The laws on inheritance, widowhood, the levirate, the rights of the poor and foreigners, and sexual "promiscuity" are burdened by the notion of "difference." The intertextuality that unites the Torah and Ruth does not allow reading Ruth except through the prism of the Torah, and vice versa, it is necessary to read the Torah through the rereading of Ruth.

The book of Ruth is as alive as the reading community. The text can "answer back," and in the process of interpretation, the interpreters are themselves interpreted. The commentator seeks to enable the text of Ruth to challenge readers. "For what reason—asks the Midrash—was the book of Ruth written? To teach us how great the reward is for those who practice *hesed* (loving kindness/goodness/ loyalty/" (Ruth Rab. 2.14). To give priority to the commandment over the Law is subversive. Respecting the letter of the Law may bring death. The audacity to consider that the faithful performance of the Law consists solely in transgressing its letter is revolutionary.

From literary and ideological standpoints, the tension between the two options is maintained in the Israelite tradition by the dynamic relationship between the *Halakah* (the "prescriptive" in the tradition) and the Haggadic (narrative). The coexistence of these two components buttresses the literary richness of the book of Ruth. What connects them here is *hesed*, in other words, that which goes beyond conventional or legislated morality. Examples of *hesed* in the book of Ruth follow one after the other. They include Ruth's devotion to her mother-in-law, the offering of herself to Boaz at the threshing floor, and Boaz's extravagant offer to marry her in the name of the *gōĕl* which by legal definition in no way includes such a marriage (see Lev 25:25–30, 47–55; Jer 32:1–15; and Num 35:12, 19–27). If readers ignore this ethical-religious context, the scene at the threshing floor and the initial recommendation of Naomi to her daughter-in-law (3:1–4) is an integral part of the plot. *Hesed* alone elevates the act of Naomi and Ruth and the reaction of Boaz from the trivial to the sublime, from the sordid to the sacred. Here again, the Law is not absent; Ruth invokes the Law when she mentions the *gōĕl* a surprising question from a Moabite. However, Ruth's declaration is soon surpassed; for if Boaz remains fastidious about the Law, nothing of what Ruth expects will come to pass. Ruth reminds Boaz that he is a man of the Law, so he may conclude that this same Law is relative! One understands Boaz's astonishment before the extreme audacity of this Moabite.

If the story had presented a man indifferent to the Law, there would be no dialectic here. The narrator characterizes Boaz throughout the story as a moral man, a principled man of a certain age. He is without impetuosity, somewhat overtaken by the events, but wise, conservative, and respectful of laws and customs. What Ruth requires from him is strange and even foreign. What changes his opinion is Ruth's *hesed*. He will accept her challenge, and thereby, he will become another man; he will go through a rebirth, signified and manifested by the birth of his son Obed. Boaz is the audience chosen by the narrator. He represents the reader of the fifth century BCE. The story is told to disorient and to reorient him towards a new view and life. In him effectively resides a real potential; however, for him to realize himself, it is necessary that he encounters Ruth the Moabite. The situation is paradoxical for, according to the Law, it is through contact with the Israelites that the gentiles learn the Law. Other Second Temple stories locate their lead characters in the Diaspora. Each of them delivers the country of his or her exile as well as its king, for example, Jonah and the king of Nineveh, Esther and the king of Persia, and Daniel and the kings of Babylon. Ruth presents the opposite position: she is the foreigner in Judah, and it is in contact with the Moabite that the Judean realizes himself. The story may be a reaction to the Ezra and Nehemiah fifth-century teaching. Ruth is a Judean book addressing Judeans; its use is internal.

However, since the audience was widened to the "nations," as early as the first century, nothing prevents readers from finding a parallel there to the message of Isaiah 55–66. The book of Ruth, like other biblical books, such as Jonah and Esther, illustrates this point of encounter. Ḥesed characterizes Ruth. Obedience to the Law is meritorious, but ḥesed surpasses personal adherence to the Law. Boaz employs ḥesed in response to Ruth's ḥesed, and one expects that the LORD extends ḥesed in return (Ruth 2:12).

The book of Ruth portrays the theme of return; the narrator reaffirms it throughout this chapter. Probably, it was a primary concern among exiles in Babylon. For Naomi, the motif is not surprising but not for Ruth. The narrator suggests that, for her, this is also a return (1:6, 22; 2:6). Ruth had not previously been to Judah and, consequently, it is illogical to say (three times) that she returned there. However, the Hebrew verb indicates physical return or repentance. Ruth, of course, does not "return" to Judah, but she turns her back on the plains of Moab; her movement is one of return. Orpah returned "to her people and her gods" (1:15). Later in the narrative, Naomi addressing Ruth describes Boaz as "our kinsman Boaz" (3:2). The figure of Orpah attracts the attention of modern feminist critics, who occasionally take the role of advocates on her behalf. Today, one may compare Ruth and Orpah to the numerous contemporary immigrants. Orpah is a model of those who do not deny their origins. Ruth remains "the Moabite" in Judah (1:22; 2:2, 6, 21; 4:5, 10). She also presents herself as a foreigner (2:10).

Ruth enters Israel prompted by her ḥesed for Naomi. She places herself beneath "the wings" of YHWH as she states herself (1:16–17); she uses the name YHWH, and her neighbours recognize it also (2:12; 3:10; 4:11–12, 14–15). Her situation is not one of passing from one culture to another with the possibility of preserving the values of Moab in Bethlehem. Orpah returns to "her gods" (1:15) and no further comments appear.[1] Structurally, she corresponds to the unnamed character in chapter 4. Ruth vowed to make Naomi's god her God. Naomi exhorts her daughters-in-law to return to their "mother's house" (1:8). When Orpah chooses this option, Naomi notes that she returned "to her gods," thus implying "security"

1. According to Num 25:2, the Israelites coming from Egypt offered sacrifices to the gods of Moab but met with hostility.

and Orpah would have understood that. Ruth chooses radical insecurity and places herself under "the wings" of Israel's God. She blesses God's people, but it is remarkable that every mention of Ruth's "return" is accompanied by "the plains of Moab."[2]

2. Perhaps a reminder of the indelible episode of the hostile attitude of the Moabites towards Israel at the time of the exodus from Egypt. The Israelite ostracism regarding the Moabites goes back to the episode on "the plains of Moab" (Deut 23:3–4).

Chapter 5

RUTH: A WOMAN OF *ḤESEḎ*

A close ecological reading of the book of Ruth reveals that Earth and the Earth community are major players and perform leading roles throughout the narrative. Traditionally, many scholars have read this story as a narrative about human loyalty or the *ḥeseḏ* of two women. When we read from an ecological perspective, we find that the narrator recounts a story about Earth's faithfulness and *ḥeseḏ*. Several pivotal themes become apparent in an ecological interpretation. The first of these is movement from the emptiness of famine, hunger, exile, and death to the fullness of fruitful harvests of grain, threshing of new grain, formation of new relationships, and the generation of new life made possible by newfound relationships with Earth, in the Earth community and in the human sphere.

A second key theme running through the Ruth narrative is how Earth and the Earth community cycle is consistently one step ahead of the human sequence. We see this exemplified several times in the narrative. Famine drives the decision of Elimelech, Naomi, and their sons, Mahlon and Chilion, to go into exile to Moab. Death then claims Elimelech. The possibility of new life surfaces with the news that the sons took Moabite wives, Orpah and Ruth, and lived in Moab for ten years (Ruth 1:4). However, this promise of new life vanishes with verse 5 stating that Mahlon and Chilion died. The bereavement of Naomi, Ruth, and Orpah emphasizes how death takes centre stage in this section of the narrative. Just as hunger, starvation, and exile mark Ruth 1:1–2, death and sterility stalk Naomi's ten-year stay in Moab—"the woman was bereft of her two sons and her husband." Thus, death ends three marriages. Such life-defying events as the bereavement and barrenness outlined in verses 1–5 suggest a story without a future (cf. 4:14–17).[1]

Ruth 1:6–13

Ruth 1:6–13 contrasts sharply with Ruth 1:6, where the narrator declares, "Then she [Naomi] arose with her daughters-in-law from Moab for she had heard that

---

1. But the death of the sons Mahlon and Chilion at the story's beginning is counterbalanced at the end by the birth of a son who holds the promise of a future, not only for the family at the centre of the narrative but for the nation of Israel also (4:14–17).

Yahweh had visited his people and given them food." Naomi's decision to return to the land of Judah signals a new beginning but the pivotal claim is that YHWH had visited his people and given them food (in Hebrew an alliterative phrase, *lātē lāhem lāhem*). This is the first of two references to the Lord's direct intervention in human life.[2] Once again, we see how news of Earth's fruitfulness or lack of it precedes and prompts human actions. Naomi exhorts her daughters-in-law to return to their mothers' house and prays that Yahweh deals kindly with them and grants each of them a home in the house of her husband. Naomi appears not to envisage security for women (v. 9) except in marriage, a thought that continues through verses 11–13. Naomi's words express hopeless despair and self-pity, if we go with "it has been far more bitter for me than for you" (*NRSV*), or altruistic concern, "it is exceedingly bitter to me for your sake" (*RSV*).[3] Whichever meaning we favour, she does not see an independent existence for her daughters-in-law and she cannot provide husbands for them. Ruth 1:16–17, which outlines Ruth's vow to accompany Naomi in life and in death, is Earth-centred—she will become one with the Earth of Judah, which is Naomi's country, in life and in death.

Ruth 1:19–22

The deficiencies of Naomi's character are evident here. She defines "full" and "empty" in verse 21 simply in terms of male relatives. In fact, she left for Moab not "full" but was fleeing from famine; she returned to Bethlehem not "empty" but assured of Ruth's enduring vow of loyalty to her. Their arrival in Bethlehem coincides with the beginning of the barley harvest (Ruth 1:22). This transition verse alerts us to the Earth's seasons, produce, and the control that Earth and Earth's activities have over the lives of human characters. From an ecological perspective, chapter 1 moves from famine in verse 1 to harvest in verse 22, from Bethlehem to Moab to Bethlehem. Throughout, it is totally Earth centred and Earth dependent.[4]

2. In both instances, YHWH acts to secure a future, first by the provision of food and second by enabling the conception of a child [4:13]. In this narrative, YHWH is the source of blessing—"may YHWH deal kindly with you" (v. 8) and Shaddai, the Almighty, of catastrophe "the Almighty has dealt bitterly with me" (v. 20).

3. We see here the ambivalence of Naomi's character—whether we hear her instruction to Ruth and Orpah as an expression of a genuine concern for their future or a despairing rejection of them as she wants them gone.

4. Pathos and irony pervade this chapter—despite Ruth's extraordinary vow of loyalty to Naomi and her God, and her choosing a future without promise or hope, Naomi ignores her as do the people of Bethlehem. The narrator designates her "Naomi returned and Ruth the Moabite" (v. 22), even though it is with her that the future lies.

Ruth 2:1-7

In 2:1–2, Naomi alludes to Boaz the wealthy kinsman and immediately Ruth makes a twofold offer to seek sustenance for herself and Naomi—"let me go to the field and glean among the ears of grain after him—I shall find favour." Ruth, still called a Moabite, hopes that Earth will sustain them in their poverty. Here she claims the right of the poor enshrined in the law to glean at harvest (Lev 19:9–10). The narrator attributes her arrival on Boaz's land to chance/luck [*miqreh*]. Boaz's question in verse 5, "to whom does this young woman belong?" reflects the assumptions of a patriarchal society. The servant identifies Ruth not by name but as a Moabite and by her relationship to Naomi. He describes her unstinting labour, her stamina, and perseverance, "without resting even for a moment."[5] "She has been on her feet ever since she came this morning."[6] "She has hardly had a moment's rest in the shelter." Ruth's closeness to Earth and her ability to "be on her feet" to be one with Earth is recognized by the workers who also toil on Earth.

Ruth 2:8–16: Earth's abundance

In Ruth's first encounter with Boaz, he commands her to remain in his field and offers her protection and advice (2:9).[7] His invitation highlights the fruits of the Earth that he offers to Ruth: "when you are thirsty go to the vessels and drink what the young men have drawn." Then she fell prostrate, with her face to the ground [*eretz*], and said to him, "Why have I found favor in your sight, that you should take notice of me, when I am a foreigner" (2:10). The combining of Yahweh's blessing and Boaz's favour in verses 2–13 is significant in the claim in verse 12 "under whose wings you have sought refuge." Boaz tells her "at mealtime come here and eat some bread and dip your morsel in the wine—he passed her parched grain and she ate, until she was satisfied, and she had some left over." Only Yahweh can pay her wages in full "full reward," but Boaz is to be the agent of this blessing for under his skirts *kanap* Ruth will eventually find security (3:9). Behind Ruth's words, "you have … spoken kindly" (literally "to speak to the heart" in verse 13) may lie some ambivalence. In some contexts, this expression denotes the gentle appeal of a lover (Hos 2:14). The narrative is rich in such ambiguities that foreshadow the conclusion of the story. The generosity of Boaz's provision for

---

5. *NRSV.*

6. *JSB.*

7. Boaz's protection of Ruth (v. 9): "I have ordered the young men not to molest you" contains echoes of the divine protection afforded to Sarah (Gen 20:6) and Rebecca (Gen 26:11). Ruth's response plays on the verb "acknowledge" and the noun "foreigner" [*nokri*], a category of persons distinct from the "resident alien" [*ger*] who had legal rights of protection within the community.

Ruth in verses 14–16 highlights the rich harvest in contrast to the starvation of a time of famine.

Ruth 2:17–23

Ruth knows how to obtain the best from her labour—she is Earth at one with the Earth and gleaned in the field until evening. She is a true Earth woman and knows to beat out what she had gleaned. She also ensures that she takes back her harvested grain to Naomi along with her leftover lunch! The end of the chapter marks the end of harvest and the beginning of a new uncertain future for both women. Where will the women find sustenance now? Naomi takes the initiative.[8]

Ruth 3:1–14

Chapter 3, unlike chapters 1 and 2, has no public aspect. It begins and ends with a private conversation between Ruth and Naomi and pivots on the intimate scene between Ruth and Boaz at the threshing floor. Ruth went down to the threshing floor and and following Naomi's instruction she lies on the earth. The man was startled and behold a woman lay at this feet—Boaz describes Ruth as a valiant woman 'ēšet ḥayil surely evoking the woman in Proverbs 31. Once more Earth provides—the darkness of night enables and witnesses the resolution of famine and lack of the means of survival with the scene at the threshing floor amidst piles of harvested grain when a vulnerable foreign woman enters a dangerous place as a supplicant.

Ruth 3:15–18

The themes of emptiness and fullness, prominent in Naomi's lament in 1:21, recur in 3:15–18. Naomi's physical emptiness/hunger is relieved, but this is but a prelude to the satisfying of her deeper need. Naomi had the first word in this chapter. Now she has the last word. Boaz's mention of the closer relative introduces an element of uncertainty into her carefully conceived plan. Once again, an element of chance or luck comes into play. In verse 18, she tells Ruth to wait and see how the matter will fall—no calling on YHWH to intervene; the emphasis is on human action and loyalty—ḥesed. As with her entry onto the threshing floor in darkness, Ruth exits from the threshing floor also under cover of darkness. Verse 14 says, "She lay at this feet until dawn" but "she rose before one person could distinguish another" (or his friend), for he said, "let it not be known that the woman came to the threshing floor." Darkness enables human actions to take place in secret, thus avoiding many problems—decisions are dependent on night and day. The light of

---

8. Verse 20 claims that Boaz is a kinsman redeemer goël (Lev 25:25, 47–49).

day illumines Ruth's emergence with a further supply of grain signals the treasure that Naomi will receive with Obed's birth and a promise of fulfilment.

Ruth 4:1–6

Action now moves back to the public sphere and to exclusively male participants engaging in the apportioning of land rights and trade-offs leading to marriage and security for women inside the city gate. In verse 5, Boaz plays his trump bargaining chip, "The day you acquire the field from the hand of Naomi you are also acquiring Ruth the Moabite." The marriage is ostensibly to maintain the dead man's name on his inheritance (vv. 5, 10).

Ruth 4:7–13

A group of elders (v. 2) and the people (v. 11) ratify the agreement concerning the property and the marriage. Significantly, the blessing (v. 1) compares Ruth to Rachel and Leah mothers to the twelve tribes, while verse 12 further associates her with Tamar, who like Ruth was a foreigner. According to Gen 38, she used unconventional means to ensure the future of a tribe threatened by extinction. Ruth is not the first foreign woman in the genealogy of the Davidic line.

Ruth 4:14–22

Now for the second time in the story, YHWH intervenes enabling Ruth to conceive. However, from verse 14 to the end, Ruth is not visible or active. The story ends as it began with Naomi empty through famine and bereaved, but now filled by the birth to a male child, Naomi's future is assured by the birth of the newborn (4:15–17). So, the text echoes what was the community belief that women still need a male *goʾel*. However the response of the women in 4:15 puts the importance of sons in perspective. Ruth's love for Naomi is of more value than seven sons. Thereafter, the focus is on Naomi and the child. The concluding genealogy is male but the book bears Ruth's name.

From a tale of famine, death, and loss, the genealogy points to a glorious future. In the canonical context, their importance lies in giving the story a wider significance than the purely domestic and in introducing the promise of hope after the despair with which the book of Judges ends.

An Earth reading

An Earth reading of Ruth offers the audience a vision of the wholeness of Earth and the Earth community. Ruth's simplicity and attractiveness as a human story masks the pivotal roles that famine, day, night, land, fields, barley harvest, wheat harvest, and threshing floor play in the narrative. The narrator depicts each of these Earth elements accomplishing its purpose in the Earth community. We realize how each human character is totally at the mercy of these Earth elements. In the course of the narrative, some human characters live and some die. The narrator embodies in the experience of each of the human characters a contrast between death and life and offers examples of what it means to "choose life" (cf. Deut 30:11–20). The flourishing or decline of Earth and the Earth community highlights the absolute dependence of human creatures on Earth and all its elements.

Many interpreters, readers, and preachers regard Ruth as a simple village story, not a universal narrative. They envision the account as an ideal on a manageable scale that they can closely relate to their own circumstances. In such interpretations, the account remains on a recognizably human plane with audiences relating to the flesh-and-blood human characters and to the picture of a human community that is far from ideal, even at a village level. An Earth interpretation enables readers to recognize the story's embodiment of a this-worldly hope sustained by a narrator who invites readers to identify with Earth and Earth's creatures in a struggle for survival. While the geographic locale and genealogy relate to David, the explicit focus of the narrative is concerned with Earth's actions rather than with divine actions.

Many interpretations of Ruth have argued that it is the brave and bold decisions of women that embody and bring to pass the blessings of God in this narrative. Such readings subordinate the role of Boaz to the activities of Ruth and Naomi in the presentation. By highlighting the human aspect of the action, we opt to focus on how the female characters escape destitution and starvation and find life and prosperity. Such readings must also address the fact that although women and men appear to work together at the end of the story, women must wring concessions and opportunities out of the dominant male, patriarchal setting in which they live. I address some of the questionable aspects of this reading later in this chapter.

Other readings focus on how God functions throughout the text or works through the human characters. However, I seek to focus on the actions of Earth and Earth's elements (famine, exile, death, barley and wheat harvests, night, etc.) in contrast to focusing on the contributions of the Deity to the positive resolution of the story. Perhaps this reading brings a different perspective and theological weight to the concluding vision of survival and fullness.

Hermeneutic of suspicion

Many have read this text as highlighting the women's power to bring fulfilment and human liberation. Nonetheless, the narrator portrays the practice of *ḥesed*, the presence of God and liberation however compromised by mixed and complicated motives, and complex relationships in the struggle for survival. Keeping in mind that Earth and Earth's surviving characters are engaged in a post-famine recovery effort, mixed motives and multifaceted relationships are at the heart of this struggle. Relationships that seek long-term survival demand physical endurance, adaptability, predictability, and credibility. They must promise stability, economic improvement, and strategies for resolving conflicts over scarce resources and ideological and symbolic differences.

Ruth is a narrative in which Earth, Earth characters, and human actors are complex and resist consideration under the single viewpoint of the omniscient narrator. Sometimes, women's contemporary concerns for freedom from patriarchy challenges and subverts any reading that praises women's altruism in service of values such as the importance of preserving the male family line presumed to be culturally masculine. Such a plausible reading is not necessarily a compelling reading.

Likewise, the character of the relationship between the two women, especially the care of the younger woman for the older, is a central component in many appropriations of the story. In many instances churches, especially male pastors, interpret this story to urge upon women their traditional role in families, a role of servant to mother-in-law that supposedly precludes work outside the home. For many younger Christian women, Ruth is an oppressive text. By contrast, the theme of women bound by economic structures, so significant for some, does not arise for others; reactions range from mystification to dismissal, as completely unimportant to enthusiastic endorsement of this angle for viewing the story. Some women even justify decisions to work abroad by invoking the example of Ruth, who left her home country for a foreign land, made contacts, entered dangerous spaces, and succeeded in winning a rich husband who supported not only herself but also her mother-in-law. They claim a belief that God will take care of them, just as God took care of Ruth. We could question Ruth's expression of loyalty to Naomi in 1:16–17 as a smokescreen that did not reveal her compelling personal reasons for leaving Moab. It is important to remember that Ruth has already married a foreigner, so her second marriage to a foreigner is not unique for her!

In assessing the final chapter of Ruth, let us consider the male-centred legal proceedings at the gate and the male-focused blessing addressed to Boaz. Some readers find a hopeful counterpoint in the women-centred closing scene. I suggest, however, the need to emphasize that the "optimistic reading" tone of chapter 4 can be sustained by the hearer only if one accepts the importance of a male heir and the customary economic arrangements of financial support through a wealthy husband as a satisfactory social structure.

The human resolution of Naomi's loss, in which the women of Bethlehem say, "A son has been born to Naomi" (4:17), highlights the unclear inheritance structures suggested in the Ruth narrative. Many women sense that this expression supports some cultural tradition that they try to resist. This appears where responsibility for child rearing belonged traditionally to the paternal or maternal grandmother; the children's mother had a subservient role in their upbringing. She was expected to be more a servant to their grandmother, her mother-in-law. Likewise, inheritance patterns may be of little interest, while worries about the role of daughters-in-law may extend far beyond questions of working outside the home. What many might regard as the joyful climax of the book can be abhorrent for some women.

A significant step in reading Ruth from an ecological perspective or reclaiming the place of Earth and of Earth elements in the Ruth narrative is a rejection of the notion that the narrative is essentially and solely about the human characters. This step is perhaps obvious to many readers, yet this hermeneutical move has larger implications. It means that we do not read this text from an ancient place and time, simply as a village story. A hermeneutical move to an ecological reading demands recognition of some critical features in this text. These include specific details of the legal system of decision making, the legal system itself, categories of inheritance, and redemption and economic structures implied by or embedded in the legal system. These all assume specific understandings of the relationships with Earth and Earth elements of the human character in the text. Use of the text to reinforce traditional relationships and patterns of family structures of contemporary cultures or use of the text to reinforce traditional patterns of economic dependence in marriage is an effort to replicate parts of the picture provided by the text without giving proper attention to the goal of the text.

If we agree that the narrator intends to provide readers with a happy conclusion, what are the underlying components of that ending, the concluding vision that ancient hearers who accepted this expression of the vision as adequate would have recognized? From an ecological perspective, the Ruth story exhibits the following components: a human community characterized by reciprocal relationship with Earth and Earth elements. Human characters are aware of their dependence on Earth and Earth's produce, that their survival demands racial and ethnic inclusiveness and adequate physical sustenance. Together, they affirm justice and mercy by caring for children and value the elderly and daughters and sons. It is these features, rather than their specific cultural expression or the specific means of achieving these ends within the story, that portray how Earth and Earth elements and creatures are portrayed.

Many have emphasized that biblical language about God is metaphorical. God is not "male." This fundamental starting point for appropriating God language has consequences for our interpretation of texts from an ecological perspective. Some have reinterpreted the text by stating its underlying themes in fresh imagery that still embody the original understanding. An Earth reading of Ruth points to a world in which Earth and Earth elements—crop failure or success, food, work, light, darkness, seasons, harvests, and other Earth elements and creatures—play a critical role. The village scale of the vision, while microcosmic and thus more readily imaginable, is not of lesser significance because of its scale.

The story of Ruth could not exist without human participants in the sense that the actions of the characters, most notably Ruth, Naomi, and Boaz but also the other men and women of the village, provide engaging characters that move the action along. In an Earth reading, the focus not only encompasses the notion of God working through Earth and all Earth creatures including the human characters but also highlights how all participate in God's work. Traditionally, many scholars have been conditioned to begin from an anthropocentric reading of texts. Consequently, as interpreters our tendency is to read from an anthropocentric viewpoint. It takes considerable effort to get to a view of the text where Earth and

Earth elements are central and pivotal rather than expecting some cataclysmic divine action.

God's involvement in the action

Once the opening verses of Ruth establish the disastrous situation of famine, flight, and death, the remainder of the story highlights two direct interventions of God towards the restoration of wholeness and community. God's provision of food in formerly famine-stricken Bethlehem (1:6) initiates the restoration as does God's enabling of the conception of Obed by Ruth (4:13) brings it to fruition. These two divine acts may represent those aspects of the natural order over which ancient peoples experienced least control. Elsewhere in Ruth, human beings call on God to do what they believe themselves unable to accomplish as we see in Naomi's prayer in Ruth 1:8: "May YHWH deal with you kindly as you have dealt with the dead." So is the narrator showing God at work behind the human actions, all of which are inseparable from Earth's ongoing momentum as experienced in famine or fruitful harvest or its failure, fertility or infertility, life or death? Naomi states an intriguing conviction in her prayer in Ruth 2:20: "Blessed be he by the Lord whose kindness has not forsaken the living or the dead—the man is a relative of ours, one of our nearest kin." So while on the one hand she offers thanks to the Lord, on the other she claims family/blood connections in the earthly sphere.

Is it random luck that Ruth went to Boaz's field, rather than elsewhere (2:3)? By the end of the story, we see Naomi's prayer commending Ruth to God's hands fulfilled through the actions of the human characters, but it would not have happened if Ruth had not gone to the field of Boaz. Human action and divine action together lead to the establishment of the happy community in Bethlehem that offers future hope. Inherent in the narrative is the lesson that we do not have to choose between God's action and our own.

The Ruth story does not present great powers of sin and evil as obstacles the characters must overcome, but the power of crop failure, famine, death, widowhood, food shortage, infertility, and lack of marriageable males is conspicuous in the story.

The place of Ruth in the structure of the Christian canon may offer a tentative link to the theme of how a community may overcome or mitigate sin and evil. Ruth begins, "In the days of the Judges there was a famine in the land." This era we know from the preceding book of Judges as one filled not just with Israelite warfare against external enemies but also with the most horrific internal struggles, murders, and destruction imaginable, devastation in which women are especially victimized (Judg 19–21). Over against such communal collapse, Ruth offers a narrative for a different way, watched over by God and initiated through an unexpected human source—a woman, a poor widow, a Moabite an outsider who hails from a despised group.

Chapter 6

RUTH: WOMEN OF WORTH

In the course of their conversation at the threshing floor (3:10–11), Boaz tells Ruth that the community knows that she is 'ēšet ḥayil. This description calls to mind Prov 31:10, where this rare phrase introduces a beautiful acrostic about 'ēšet ḥayil, the "valiant/worthy woman." This is the final poem in the book of Proverbs.[1] Boaz's description of Ruth as 'ēšet ḥayil follows close on his "do not be afraid" assurance to Ruth suggesting how great a risk Ruth has taken in approaching him by night and making her proposal. He could have taken advantage physically or declined her proposal or questioned her integrity by letting the village know about the episode. Boaz's agreement to her request and his affirmation of her excellent reputation confirms his awareness of her courage and her reasons to be afraid. However, there is no indication that Ruth is afraid, so why does Boaz tell her not to fear when he was the one who showed fear on the threshing floor? In telling Ruth not to fear, Boaz may be attempting to retake the decision making. Ruth has little to lose other than Boaz's devotion and it seemed unlikely that she would suffer the loss of his care for her at this stage. Now Boaz refers to Ruth as 'ēšet ḥayil, "woman of "strength" or "virtue" or "worthy woman" (NRSV). In 2:1, the narrator calls Boaz "a man of "strength" or "virtue" or "prominent rich man." This phrase recalls the "woman of strength" or "virtue" or "valiant woman" in Proverbs where the translators use "good wife" (Prov 12:4) and "capable wife" (Prov 31:12) in the NRSV. The "strong," "virtuous," or "valiant" woman is characterized by her capabilities in providing for the entire household, buying land, planting her vineyard, spinning and weaving, selling merchandise in the market, and ensuring adequate food for the household while also providing stretching out her hands to the poor and needy. In contrast, Boaz the landowner calls Ruth 'ēšet ḥayil, "woman of strength," when she is migrant childless widow who gleans in his barley field to obtain enough grain to feed herself and Naomi. The narrator uses ḥayil when speaking of male characters who are "strong," "able-bodied" (Judg 3:29), or a man of "wealth" (1 Sam 9:1), which echoes the description of Boaz in Ruth 2:1. Often ḥayil appears when the writer refers to armies, for example, "warrior" (Josh 6:2; 8:3; 10:7; Judg 6:12; 11:1).

---

1. The NRSV translates ēšet ḥayil as "capable wife" in Prov 31:10.

The 'ēšet ḥayil in Prov 31 has attracted a variety of judgements from scholars concerning her identity. Many commentators argue that the 'ēšet ḥayil, the "woman of worth," is a depiction of personified Wisdom and that Prov 31:10–31 completes depictions of personified Wisdom in Prov 1–9. Many who propose this scenario overlook the many human characteristics of the idealized, earthly woman/wife. The 'ēšet ḥayil, the central character in Prov 31:10–31, is, in all respects, the opposite of the wicked women depicted in Prov 1–9. She embodies the "good woman," the essential spouse for any man seeking a wise wife and would fulfil male aspirations regarding family, physical strength, efficient household management, business acumen, profit-making abilities, and a sterling reputation.

There are many descriptions of what makes for good or bad women throughout biblical wisdom literature. Prov 1–9 feature "bad" women as represented by "the foreign woman /adventurer /the woman whose husband is away" as opposed to personified Wisdom. From the third millennium BCE, this topic appeared in Egyptian and Babylonian instructions, generally concerning marriage. The choice between Wisdom and Folly is also significant in wisdom literature, with Proverbs providing lurid "wicked women" characters who are purveyors of temptations to infidelity, sexual deviance, and deceit countered by images of personified Wisdom offering life.

It is not surprising that the book of Ruth reads validly as a wisdom text since we find it in the *Tanakh*, in the third section of the Hebrew canon, traditionally designated "The Writings" (Ketuvim). Ruth is part of a set of five "Festival Scrolls" Megillot: Song of Songs, Ruth, Lamentations, Qoheleth (Ecclesiastes), and Esther. Devout Jews read Ruth during the Feast of Weeks because of its association with the harvest season (cf. Lev 23:15–21; Num 28:26–31). While the tradition of placing Ruth among the Writings is attested as early as first-century CE, the collection of the five festival scrolls as a group may have happened several centuries later. The order of these five scrolls varies with one based on the annual sequence of festivals, and another based on the place of each book in the chronology of Israel's history. In Christian canons, the book of Ruth appears among the historical books after the book of Judges connecting it to the opening line: "In the days when the Judges ruled" (Ruth 1:1). This era places the Ruth narrative in a historical setting featuring warfare, violence, and mayhem, while Ruth features the town of Bethlehem, peasant farming, harvesting grain and the like, and traditional legal proceeding at the town gate. The book of Judges ends with an escalation of violence, warfare, murder, and bloodshed. When warfare had destroyed most members of Benjamin's tribe except for six hundred men, some victors regretted that the Benjaminites might cease to have progeny (Judg 21:6); they decide to procure wives for the survivors by the kidnapping of women. Thus by death and destruction and hostage-taking, they sought to continue a family line.

In Ruth, the theme of preserving a family line also appears in 4:5, 10. In this instance, the problem was a scarcity of men rather than women. In Ruth, however, those involved solve the problem not by murder but by courageous and carefully planned strategies dreamed up by women who were wholly concerned with human survival and how care for those with little or no means of survival rather than the preservation of a family line. The narrative depicts an eligible wealthy male citizen's willingness to marry a foreign migrant widow with a dependent mother-in-law. She has no material assets other than her willingness to glean in harvest time to support herself and her mother-in-law, to engage in a dangerous midnight tryst, marry an older man, and accept whatever the future promised.

Boaz responds to Ruth's threshing floor visit

Chapter 3:1–6 introduces Naomi's detailed instructions to Ruth concerning how to prepare and how to behave for a night-time visit to Boaz at his threshing floor. "Observe the place where he lies; then, go and uncover his feet and lie down; and he will tell you what to do." The narrator amplifies Boaz's instruction to Ruth: "lie down until morning." So the tension between sexual attraction and upright behaviour is brought full circle. She said to her, "All that you tell me I will do." So she went down to the threshing floor and did just as her mother-in-law had instructed her. Boaz turns over or twists around to see the form of a woman, though he does not recognize her in the darkness. Ironically, Ruth's physical preparations at Naomi's behest serve no purpose as they meet in midnight darkness.

In chapter 2:5, Boaz asked a male servant in the barley field about Ruth's identity, "To whom does this young woman belong?" In this night-time scene in chapter 3, Boaz, on awakening and sensing a person near him, asks directly of the figure he sees dimly, "Who are you?"[2] Ruth's responds directly to Boaz's question with, "I am Ruth, your servant; spread your cloak over your servant, for you are next-of-kin," thus deviating from Naomi's plan (3:9). However, it seems Ruth reads the situation to her advantage as Boaz responds, "May you be blessed by the LORD, my daughter; this last instance of your loyalty is better than the first; you have not gone after young men, whether poor or rich … do not be afraid, I will do for you all that you ask, for all the assembly of my people know that you are 'ēšet ḥayil a 'woman of worth'" (3:10–11). The term "going after" suggests sexual intent. The only reference to Boaz advanced years appears in 2:5, perhaps a suggestion that Ruth might have preferred a younger spouse. Did Boaz wonder if his age might be a disincentive for Ruth to pursue him? Boaz indicates his belief that Ruth acts out of *ḥesed* loyalty to Naomi. The juxtaposition of "poor or rich" suggests a toss-up between sexual attraction and economic security. Strangely, Boaz overlooks or maybe elects to be silent about the fact of his wealthy status. We do not know his age! Is Ruth pursuing material gain—why not—she has known destitution? Boaz describes her act of loyalty/loving kindness *ḥesed* as even better than her acts of

---

2. Jennifer Koosed argues that Boaz's questions about Ruth's identity indicate his unease and doubt in chapters 2–3. See Jennifer Koosed, *Gleaning Ruth: A Biblical Heroine and Her Afterlives*, Studies on Personalities of the Old Testament (Columbia: University of South Carolina Press, 2011), 2.

leaving Moab to accompany Naomi to Bethlehem and gleaning in the barley field to gather grain to feed them both: "may you have a full reward from the LORD, the God of Israel, under whose wings you have come for refuge!" (2:11–12). Although Ruth is in control of the situation, she evokes scenarios described in Prov 1–9 of wicked women (Prov 5:3–6; 6:24–26; 7:5–26) and foreign women who dress like prostitutes and prey on young men in the night.

Ruth referred to herself as Boaz's servant in 2:7, but at the threshing floor, she uses her name, unsurprisingly as she and Boaz are already acquainted.[3] She asks Boaz to spread his cloak over her, perhaps reminding Boaz of his blessing in 2:7.[4] Now Ruth shifts the responsibility by reminding Boaz if he wants to speak of the Lord's refuge; he should be prepared to act as an agent. Is Ruth proposing marriage here, or is she more subtle, warning him not to see her as a sexual object? On the threshing floor, Ruth's plan is unconventional and direct. However, survival demands action. Ruth needs action on behalf of Naomi and herself. As in 2:12, "May the LORD reward you for your deeds, and may you have a full reward from the LORD, the God of Israel, under whose wings you have come for refuge!" Boaz again invokes the Lord's blessing and calls Ruth "my daughter." He instructs her: "do not go to glean in another field" (2:8). Here he expands the image of paternal protection. The expression heightens the sense of Boaz's concern for Ruth and maybe obscures his sexual intent. After their encounter in 2:2, Boaz ensured Ruth's safety in the barley field, instructing her to help herself to the water provided by the male servants, to keep close to his female servants in the field, and he shared his meal and wine with her. Here again, Boaz takes Ruth under his protection. He cites this "last instance" of her loyalty as even more significant than the first, that is, leaving her family and homeland to accompany Naomi to Bethlehem. Her loyalty to Naomi continued when she followed her direction to go to the threshing floor under cover of darkness to meet Boaz and request that he acts as *go'el* for them both. In both cases, Ruth acts out *ḥesed* to Naomi.[5] Both acts of loyalty move Boaz to call for the Lord's blessing on Ruth.

The reality, however, is that Boaz's invoking the Lord's blessing on Ruth when he can fulfil her request is ironic. Ruth's acts of *ḥesed* to Naomi are also

---

3. For a discussion of slave and servant see Alice L. Laffey and Mahri Leonard-Fleckman, *Ruth: Wisdom Commentary* (Collegeville: Liturgical Press, 2017), 76–79. Katharine D. Sakenfeld, *The Meaning of Hesed in the Hebrew Bible: A New Inquiry*, HSM, vol. 17 (Missoula MT: Scholars Press, 1978), 57–58.

4. See Ezek 16:8: "I spread the edge of my cloak over you and covered your nakedness." On the relationship between Ruth and Ezek 16:8–10, see Jack M. Sasson, *Ruth: A New Translation with a Philological Commentary and a Formalist-Folklorist Interpretation*, 2nd ed. (Sheffield: Sheffield Academic, 1995), 66. In Ruth 3:11, the reference to wing here echoes Boaz blessing on Ruth in the barley field. "May the LORD reward you for your deeds, and may you have a full reward from the LORD, the God of Israel, under whose wings you have come for refuge!" (Ruth 2:12).

5. Sakenfeld, *The Meaning of Hesed in the Hebrew Bible*, 42–43.

qualities that she has offered Boaz that he may recognize from this point onwards. While Boaz highlights Ruth's loyalty, there may be other factors driving Ruth's behaviour on the threshing floor. Boaz's wealth may be more important than his age in Ruth's view. She may decide to choose Boaz because of his earlier demonstrations of kindness. Ruth may also have detected his interest in her, so she was already considering him as a suitable husband. Her pursuit of Boaz may have coincided with Naomi's decision that Boaz should be prevailed upon to act as *go'el*; otherwise, she would hardly have taken matters into her own hands on the threshing floor. However, other motivations may also have prompted Ruth's actions. In verse 11, Boaz responds to Ruth by echoing her words to Naomi in 3:5, "I will do for you all you ask," while Boaz stresses his concern for her well-being alone and excludes Naomi by using the singular. Throughout this scene, Ruth acts on her and Naomi's behalf, but Boaz acts for himself and Ruth. Maybe Boaz is swayed by Ruth's forcefulness in urging him to action and decision while Naomi is physically absent.

In the *Tanakh*, the book of Ruth follows the book of Proverbs. Each scroll lauds the *'ēšet ḥayil*. Ruth is in the same category as the woman of Prov 31:10. There is irony in this description of Ruth since she may also evoke images of the foreign woman or seductress in Prov 1–9 contrasted with the woman of virtue or with Wisdom. In Proverbs, all female characters are sexualized but not in the book of Ruth. The foreign woman tempts young man away from Wisdom and knowledge of God and towards death (Prov 2:16–19), while Wisdom (Prov 8), the woman of strength (Prov 31), and the wife (Prov 5) represent appropriate desire that tempts the young men towards knowledge, life, and fear of the Lord. Ruth's Moabite origin prevents her from entirely escaping the stereotype of the dangerous woman, even as Boaz relabels her as a woman of strength.

Boaz calls Ruth a "woman of worth" because he judges her actions on the threshing floor as admirable despite the sexual overtones. Although he does not state that coming to the threshing floor was among these kind acts, he never recounts the threshing floor scene publicly. Boaz's declaration of Ruth's sterling reputation among all the assembly, literally "at the gate of my people" in verse 11, further elevates her reputation as men are arbiters of good women. It is men who make the decisions in the town and determine that it will not only be Boaz who determines Ruth's suitability as a wife.[6] Instead, it is the men as well as public opinion that Ruth must convince of her suitability.

Finally, Boaz affirms that he is the *go'el* for Naomi and discloses a second "closer" *go'el* than himself. The root is then repeated six times in verses 12–13. Suddenly, Ruth has two possibilities for redemption. Boaz vows three times that he will redeem Ruth (v. 13), thus reminding the reader of the distance between Naomi and Boaz in the narrative. We see that Boaz is concerned with Ruth while keeping his own needs to the fore as he tells Ruth if the other man will act as the *go'el* that is acceptable for him but if he refuses Boaz pledges with an oath to the

---

6. Edward F. Campbell, *Ruth. AB 7* (New York: Doubleday, 1975), 124.

Lord that he will act as *go'el* for Ruth. The ease with which he discusses the other *go'el* suggests that Boaz is sure that he has persuaded Ruth to be his wife.

Likewise, the author of Proverbs attributes to the *'ēšet ḥayil*, the female figure in Prov 31:10–31, noble qualities and awe-inspiring activities of an ideal wife, from a male perspective. This faithful wife is a skilled household manager, a businesswoman, and much more, who holds centre stage both in the home and in the business community, while mention of her husband appears only in verses 23 and 28. Camp proposes that the female figure in Prov 31:10–31 is not just a portrait of an ideal woman but also represents "a universal type of wisdom." She examines the *'ēšet ḥayil* in the light of the Wisdom figure in Proverbs whom she sees as based on actual Israelite women, rather than on any Near Eastern goddess. Sayings regarding women's roles reflect the "kingless sociological configuration of the post-exilic era," when the family in some respects replaced the monarchy as the "defining element" in society.[7] Thus, the *'ēšet ḥayil* transformed, for a later audience who had no king, the royal imagery of Prov 8. While Camp's theory has found some acceptance, her interpretation of the *'ēšet ḥayil* "woman of worth" as another portrayal of Wisdom overlooks the human attributes of this character by calling them qualities of Wisdom.

From a human standpoint, the *'ēšet ḥayil* is a diligent household manager (31:21, 27) who also engages, without male mediation or interference, in profit-making ventures outside the home (vv. 16, 24). In addition, she is a wise speaker and teacher (v. 26), rather than as stay-at-home housewife or silent spouse so cherished in the ancient world and in many traditional cultures today. The *'ēšet ḥayil* goes out to engage in business, continues to see that her household runs smoothly, and cares for the poor and needy who approach her for assistance (v. 22). Ruth, as *'ēšet ḥayil*, is among the poor who have little power or influence, but she is willing to work as a gleaner while the barley and wheat harvests continue. This earthwork enables her to procure grain—put bread on the table—for herself and Naomi.

The *'ēšet ḥayil* of Prov 31:10–31 is the central character in a carefully structured acrostic. The poet uses the standard Hebrew alphabet to depict the woman's characteristics in two equal sections: *aleph* to *vav* (31:10–20) and *lamed* to *tav* (31:21–31) with 23 + 23 = 46 cola to form a dynamic acrostic. Most verses are of two lines in length with two verses of three lines each. Tricolons, which appear at the beginning (v. 10), middle (v. 20), and end (v. 31), determine the stanzas and set off verses 19–20, the *chiasm*—a perfectly balanced, self-contained unit at the centre of the poem:

31:19 She puts her **hands** to the distaff, and her **hands** hold the spindle.
31:20 She opens her **hand** to the poor and reaches out her **hands** to the needy.

---

7. Claudia V. Camp, *Wisdom and the Feminine in the Book of Proverbs*, BL 11 (Sheffield: Almond Press, 1985), 262–65, 290.

The complex composition highlights the household activities and outdoor occupations of the *'ēšet ḥayil* with her hands-on care for the poor and needy.

Thus, the poet portrays the woman as the epitome of the golden mean so lauded in wisdom teachings. Word repetition, for example, "hands" along with changes and developments in meaning, shows a tightly balanced skilfully structured acrostic poem:

31:13 She seeks wool and flax and works with willing **hands**.

31:16 She considers a field and buys it; with the fruit of her **hand,** she plants a vineyard.

31:19 She puts her **hands** to the distaff, and her **hands** hold the spindle.

31:20 She opens her **hand** to the poor and reaches out her **hands** to the needy.

31:31 Give her a share in the fruit of her **hands**, and let her works praise her in the city gates.

31:10 A capable wife who can find? She is far more precious than jewels.

31:11 The heart of her husband trusts in her, and he will have no lack of gain.

31:28 Her children rise up and call her happy; her husband too, and he praises her.

31:29 Many women have done excellently, but you surpass them all.

Prov 31:10–31 consists of seven vignettes, each revealing unique facets of the *'ēšet ḥayil* that contribute to a stunning portrait of one of the most amazing female characters in the *Tanakh*. The book of Ruth likewise provides a unique portrait of a female migrant widow who navigates powerlessness, poverty, widowhood, and childlessness. She, by the work of her hands and her courage by daylight and darkness, finds food for herself and her mother-in-law, a husband, security, and a permanent place to live in a foreign land and progeny that make her the ancestor of King David.

Vignette 1: Prov 31:10–12

In this first vignette, the association of *ḥayil* "strength" with *'ēšet* "woman" is interesting as this term, with its military connotations, is more usually applied to men in the Bible, as in "a mighty man" or "mighty warrior," "men of valour," and "valiantly" (Judg 6:12; 11:1; 2 Sam 17:10; 1 Chr 5:18; Ps 60:12). Boaz tells Ruth that she is *'ēšet ḥayil* (Ruth 3:11), and Prov 31:10 speaks of the *'ēšet ḥayil* who is a rare find. Both are characters of worth, virtue, ability, strength, vigour, power, and resourcefulness. Verse 10, "Who can find?" introduces the notion of a search, a common motif in wisdom writing. We could read the question as suggesting a futile search, as Eccl 7:24 suggests, but when considered along with Prov 12:4, which reads like a summary version of this poem, a more optimistic notion of a rarity rather than impossibility may be entertained. With its undertones of frustration and doubt in the search for an ideal wife/woman, this question probably addresses young unmarried men or women. It seems most likely that the author intends the poem for a male audience as this first vignette goes on to highlight and intensify motifs of rarity, value, and uniqueness by allusions to corals, jewels, or pearls (v. 10b). Since a significant aspect of the value of jewels and pearls derives from their scarcity and the difficulty associated with finding them, in the ancient world it is not surprising that the poet associates both qualities with the *'ēšet ḥayil*.[8] Implied in the rare jewel-like qualities of the *'ēšet ḥayil* is her inestimable value to her husband in verses 11–12, and the guarantee of a secure and prosperous life for any man who succeeds in finding such a woman. Verse 11 suggests "spoil" or "booty taken in war," but it might also be "gain" in this passage or may be metaphorical in keeping with "she does him good and not harm."[9] The portrayal of the woman as a gift to her husband's security and public advancement is a genuinely astonishing affirmation in a patriarchal society.

Vignette 2: Prov 31:13–15

In the second vignette, it is not surprising that the *'ēšet ḥayil* seeks wool and flax since she provides clothing for her household and sells her handicrafts undoubtedly made from the same raw material. She is competent and gifted, delighting in her handiwork. Dahood's translation, "She carefully seeks wool and flax, which her hands turn into a work of beauty," captures its essence (v. 13).[10] The highlighting of her skills with flax and wool places her in the company of many ancient women and emphasizes her wisdom. Next, the poet lauds her ability in obtaining and distributing food for her household and the needy. Such competence shows her to be a far-seeing and generous provider who exemplifies the prudence and careful management associated with the wise in Proverbs.

References to her "house" or "household" in verses 15, 21, and 27 highlight the woman's setting. As the poet portrays her skills as a cultivator, producer, trader, and even a merchant ship, we never lose sight of her close relationship with Earth and Earth's generosity that reminds us also of how futile her activities in a time of famine would be. She explores beyond her home context to obtain food from abroad. References to her husband's work, other than his presence "at the gates," are lacking. There is a close connection between the *'ēšet ḥayil* in verses 14–15,

---

8. Personified Wisdom describes herself as "more precious than jewels" (Prov 3:15) and "better than jewels" (Prov 8:11). We note, however, that Wisdom, who is the speaker in these texts, claims that her instruction and knowledge outclass silver and gold. These descriptions seem similar, but the contexts hold different emphases.

9. The term also occurs in Prov 16:19 in the sense of "divide the spoil." This term, with its military connotations of the victors becoming wealthy through war, seems to denote wealth here. It appears also in Isa 53:12: "he shall divide the spoil." The poem suggests that this refers to the wife's admirable skill as a manager of the household.

10. Parallel images appear in Livy, Jerome, and in Claudia's Epitaph, suggesting that spinning wool was an esteemed womanly occupation in antiquity.

who performs a daily routine of providing food and tasks for her household, and her rising before daylight to give food to her servants. This verse may suggest her concern for her servants' welfare coupled perhaps with her desire to supervise and forestall potential wastefulness. If "food" is understood as a corruption of "task," this text could indicate that she rises early to allocate her servants their tasks for the day.

Vignette 3: Prov 31:16–18

Having established how the '*ēšet ḥayil* begins her daily routine, the poet moves the scene to the outdoors where her interest and expertise in land and its cultivation add to her other accomplishments. Verse 16 describes her wise judgement in acquiring land for cultivation, and her sharp eye for business opportunities, thus showing her to be a planter of vines. Verse 17, "She girds her loins with strength and makes her arms strong," presents an image of the woman's strength as she prepares to engage in strenuous activity. It also suggests the age-old image of a woman tucking up a garment with a belt or scarf in preparation for demanding physical work.[11] The poet, by linking this phrase with the woman, places her in the company of those who participate in sacred rituals and recalls the preparation demanded of Elijah, Elisha, Job, Jeremiah, and Nahum, whom the Lord called to carry out tasks. While the work for which the '*ēšet ḥayil* "girds her loins with strength" may be spinning and weaving, attending to her household, trading, buying land, planting and tending vines, and reaching out to the poor and needy, her preparation places her activity in the realm of activity directed by God.

The poet follows the depiction of physical preparation for sustained work, during the hours of daylight, now shifts to a night-time image suggested by "her lamp does not go out" (v. 18). It may mean that the woman discerns trading conditions to be good, and so works through the night, to take full advantage of the market, which would be consistent with the emphasis on her strength and indefatigable industry.[12] The lighted lamp may signify an inhabited house, while a lack of light denotes a deserted house. If oil were a precious commodity, a lighted lamp would show the household's prosperity, since a lighted house is likely to be safe from attack, and is a welcome sight for the homeless, the traveller, and the needy of whom we hear in the next stanza.

---

11. The LXX adds "for work." An alternative phrasing could be "summons the strength of her arms," an idea expressed in Amos 2:14 and Nah 2:1. The verse echoes actions associated with males, for example, performance of ritual (Exod 12:11), prophetic actions (1 Kgs 18:46; 2 Kgs 4:29; 9:1); and people commissioned to take action (Job 38:3; 40:7; Jer 1:17; Nah 2:1).

12. It is unlikely that the expression "her lamp does not go out" (v. 18) signifies the woman's righteousness, nor can it be connected to the other biblical references which denote the putting out of the lamp of the wicked (Prov 13:9; 20:20; 24:20; Job 18:6; 21:17).

Vignette 4: Prov 31:19–21

She puts her hands to the distaff, and her hands hold the spindle.[20] She opens her hand to the poor and reaches out her hands to the needy.[21] She is not afraid for her household when it snows, for all her household are clothed in crimson. The chiasmus between verses 19 and 20 centres on the words "hands" and "hand," and includes a repetition of the verb "holds" and "reaches out" a switch in meaning in verse 20. Just as "hands" and "hand" exchange places, so they no longer refer to the woman's skills and enterprise in practical matters, but to her care for the poor and needy. She uses the "distaff" and "spindle," which suggests that she spins wool and flax (v. 19). We see here a significant development in the characterization of the woman from one who spins, weaves, and takes advantage of the market to include care for the poor and needy. The author effects this unfolding through the image of the woman's hands.

Vignette 5: Prov 31:22–24

Verse 21 has the 'ēšet ḥayil attending to the needs of her household, so she does not fear the coming of winter as she clothes her household "in scarlet" or "in double garments." Her wealth suggests that she would use the best and warmest fabric for her servants' winter clothing rather than provide multiple garments. The 'ēšet ḥayil spins wool, so she has ready access to the raw material to produce coverlets (v. 22) that protect her household against the cold throughout the night. Her husband presides in a setting that befits the spouse of 'ēšet ḥayil, and her success and good name guarantee his status. By her working both within the household and in the commercial community, the 'ēšet ḥayil makes goods and sells them to merchants. The garments are made of linen, which shows that the 'ēšet ḥayil is not only an efficient household manager, wife, and businesswoman but also an accomplished craftswoman and merchant endowed with all the virtues of the wise person according to Proverbs. While the author alluded to her clothing earlier (v. 22), here her garments are qualities associated with an authority figure. Her outward appearance denotes a role of leadership and prosperity while she is also a mother. Verse 28 mentions her children. She is concerned "for her household" (v. 21). She "speaks with wisdom" and "teaching of loving kindness" is "on her tongue" (v. 26).[13] She has prepared well for winter by building up ample supplies

---

13. Carol Meyers, "To Her Mother's House," in *The Bible and the Politics of Exegesis*, ed. D. Jobling, P. L. Day, and G. T. Sheppard (Cleveland, OH: Pilgrim, 1991), 48, notes that the phrase "teaching of loving-kindness" picks up on the association of the mother with instruction, "your mother's teaching," found in Prov 1:8; 6:20, 23; J. H. Otwell, *And Sarah Laughed: The Status of Women in the Old Testament* (Philadelphia, PA: Fortress, 1977), 108, claims that the motif of the wise wife reflected a commonplace reality in ancient Israelite culture.

of food, and ensuring that her household is warmly accoutred, so she faces the future laughingly. Verse 25 returns to the notion of "strength" with its military connotations as in verses 10 and 29. In this context, the word implies that the woman exercises these qualities with skill, dignity, and strength, while also teaching wisdom and loving kindness. Considering the scope and variety of her work, the extent of her household and business management, her physical ability, stamina, and energy, it is fitting that the poet attributes strength and valour to this character.

Vignette 6: Prov 31:25–27

In saying that the 'ēšet ḥayil banishes the "bread of idleness" from her house (v. 27) and speaks with wisdom and compassion, the author makes a clear connection between her wisdom and loving kindness, and her care for her household. As this vignette is clearly concerned with speech and the use of the tongue, topics addressed not only in Proverbs but throughout wisdom literature, the bread of idleness here alludes to idle talk, destructive speech, and gossip, all marks of the unwise and proscribed in the woman's household (cf. v. 15). As many qualities and activities attributed to the 'ēšet ḥayil are those enjoined on all who seek to be wise, it is not surprising that this vignette enumerates the praise bestowed on her by those who know and experience her gifts. Beginning the litany of praise, her children "rise up and call her blessed," and her husband, who has been mentioned but twice (vv. 11, 23), "sings her praises." To his praise is added the extended praise of the author, or the husband, or both (v. 29): "you surpass them all." This is surely the highest recognition that a husband can give to his wife. It may also be praise by the author and the audience. Verse 29 lauds the achievements of "many women," emphasising the common ground shared by the 'ēšet ḥayil and the many other women who have "done excellently."

Vignette 7: Prov 31:28–30

Concluding the litany of praise is the enigmatic: "charm is deceitful and beauty is vain, in a woman the fear of the Lord is to be praised." Much debate surrounds the meaning of this verse.[14] The point seems to be that charm and beauty are ephemeral and so can be misleading. This apparent warning about the transitory nature of appearances and beauty offers an antithesis in the second half, namely, that the woman is to be praised, not because of her beauty but because of her uprightness.[15]

14. The LXX has a double reference: "for it is an intelligent woman that is blessed and let her praise the fear of the Lord." The textual background for this reading is unclear.

15. R. N. Whybray, *The Composition of the Book of Proverbs* (Sheffield: JSOT Press, 1994), 154–6, notes that verse 30 is unlikely to be a later editorial insertion, as such a change

The much-debated reference to her "fear of the Lord," considered by some to be a later emendation to the text, hinges on its problematic syntax, its explicit and only reference to YHWH in this poem, and its unusual length. The acrostic form precludes the likelihood that the text was subject to major editorial changes or to later scribal glosses. Becker comments that "fear of YHWH" sayings are embedded in the poems about women in Proverbs (Prov 1:29; 8:13; 31:30) and "the work thus receives an inclusion or a bracketing through the motif of the fear of the Lord."[16]

Doubts concerning the inclusion of "fear of the Lord" arise from the mistaken view that sacred and secular were two quite separate spheres in the thought of the ancient world. Such a division was not likely to have been operating in the world in which Prov 31:1–31 emerged, where life experience was not compartmentalized. Lauding the woman for her practical, artistic, creative, and business skills, the very qualities named in Proverbs as the characteristics of the wise, the poet, not surprisingly, credits her with the hallmark of the wise person, "the fear of the Lord," an expression that has many biblical precedents. It occurs, with various nuances, throughout wisdom literature, as in "the fear of the Lord is hatred of evil" (Prov 8:13); "the beginning of wisdom (is) the fear of YHWH" (Prov 9:10); "the fear of YHWH is instruction in Wisdom" (Prov 15:33); "a woman who fears the Lord is to be blessed" (Prov 31:30); "the fear of the Lord that is wisdom" (Job 28:28); and "the beginning of wisdom is the fear of the Lord" (Sir 1:14).[17]

would have demanded further alterations to retain the alphabetic ordering of the poem. G. Boström, *Proverbiastudien. Die Weisheit und das fremde Weib in Spr. 1–9* (Lund: Gleerup, 1935), claims that while it is through the phrase "fear of YHWH" that Wisdom is brought into relationship with Yahweh-religion, this does not have cultic implications in the book of Proverbs but suggests an ethical orientation. Cf. J. Becker, *Gottesfurcht im Alten Testament*, AnBib 25 (Rome: Pontifical Biblical Institute, 1963), 210–41.

16. Becker, *Gottesfurcht*, 21; C. H. A. Toy, *A Critical and Exegetical Commentary of the Book of Proverbs* (Edinburgh: T & T Clark, 1899), 548; and Otto Plöger, *Sprüche Salomos* (Neukirchen-Vluyn: Neukirchener Verlag), 379, claimed that since this is purely a "secular" poem, the brief reference to the fear of YHWH is incongruous and cannot be original (cf. Job 28:28).

17. Some studies of "fear of God/Lord" in the Old Testament note the origin of the idea in the human reaction to the numinous. See S. Plath, *Furcht Gottes* (Stuttgart: Calwer, 1962); Becker, *Gottesfurcht*; L. Derousseau, *La crainte de Dieu dans l'Ancien Testament* (LD; Paris: Éditions du Cerf, 1970); M. L. Barré, "'Fear of God' and the World of Wisdom" *BTB* 11 (1981), 41–43, notes that fear of God or gods is "a common concept in all areas of the ancient Near East, a concept moreover which is regularly encountered in the wisdom literature of this region." It seems most likely that "knowledge"(Prov 1:7a) was the original word used since it is unlikely that "knowledge" would have been substituted for "wisdom" later; Camp, *Wisdom*, 96, maintains that a later editor saw parallels between the figures of Wisdom (8:13) and the "worthy woman" (v. 30), so saw fit to attribute "fear of YHWH" to both characters.

Although it may be glossed, a strong moral connotation is attached to "fear of the Lord" (8:13), and the same meaning may be intended in Prov 3:7, where fear is associated with turning away from moral evil. Clearly, the "fear of the Lord" is the touchstone of genuine wisdom, so its placement in 8:13 is in harmony with a list of Wisdom's attributes. Likewise, its absence or rejection brings the consequences implied in "they will eat the fruit of their way" (1:31–32).[18] It must also be noted that a line of unusual length in a poem, which is otherwise regular in meter, can be a deliberate device to indicate the conclusion of a stanza or poem, signalling a climax or denoting emphasis.[19] In this case, verse 30, far from being a token religious reference, out of tune with Prov 31:10–31 as a whole, is the climax of the poem. The length may emphasize the importance, and comprehensiveness of the woman's virtues, while simultaneously changing pace to bring the list to completion.

Closing acclamation (Prov 31:31)

It is surprising to hear human works praised as in verse 31: "her works praise her in the city gates." In the Psalter, we hear God's works praised and thanks rendered to the One who accomplishes them (Ps 145:10; 19:1–4), and thanksgiving that the "fruit of YHWH's work" satisfies the Earth (Ps 104:13; cf. Prov 31:31). It is possible that the imperative in verse 31, "Give her of the fruit of her hands," follows a hymn form used in works for performance in public.[20] This last verse commanding praise for the *'ēšet ḥayil* who "fears the Lord" is like a conclusion to a litany where the final accolade portrays her as the embodiment of characteristics integral to Wisdom in Proverbs: "The fear of the Lord is the beginning of knowledge" (1:7).[21] To praise the *'ēšet ḥayil* "at the gates" (v. 31) is to praise her in the place where her husband sits but more importantly she is praised in the place where the elders preside and give judgement. We must therefore conclude that she is awarded praise in justice and on her own merits. Augustine devoted his *Sermo* 37 to the "valiant woman" and was emulated by Gregory the Great and the Venerable Bede.[22] Albert the Great contributed a book on Prov 31:10–31 in which he presented his

18. R. E. Murphy, "Religious Dimensions of Israelite Wisdom," in *Ancient Israelite Religion*, ed. P. D Miller, P. D. Hanson, and S. Dean McBride (Philadelphia, PA: Fortress,1987), 458, n. 17, notes that only in Israel do we find an explicit and intimate association of wisdom with "fear of God."

19. See W. Baumgartner, "Die israelitische Weisheitsliteratur," *ThR* 5 (1933), 277; and Whybray, *Proverbs* (1994), 155.

20. Berend Gemser, *Sprüche Salomos* (Tübingen: Mohr, 1963), 110, proposes, "Give her praise for the fruit of her hands."

21. In Sir 44–49, the author reads Proverbs with a different spirit so praises "Fathers."

22. "Sermones de Vetere Testamento" (CC 41: 446–73); Gregory did not do a commentary on Proverbs but used an allegorical interpretation of Prov 31:10–31 in his writings.

allegorical exegesis of this poem. From Origen to the Reformation, and until much later in the Catholic tradition, allegorical interpretation was the accepted position. Scholars of recent decades who see Prov 31:10–31 as Wisdom seem unaware of the patristic precedent for their view.

ʾēšet ḥayil: Aleph to Taw woman

The author of Prov 31:10–31, by using the acrostic form, signals something akin to "a complete list" or an "Aleph to Taw" summary of the combined qualities and achievements that distinguish the "woman of worth," and thus identify the kind of woman the wise man must seek as his wife. This acrostic combines many functions of acrostics outlined above, such as easing memorization, an enhancing attribute if the poem is to be recited, chanted, or sung in unison. Since alphabetical order is an integral feature of the acrostic, Prov 31:10–31 could function like a checklist that enumerates the activities and qualities of the ideal wife, and thus assists recall and enumeration of the characteristics outlined in the poem. Perhaps the very characteristics, which some scholars have seen as demanding an inconsistent order, are the result of deliberate placement and designed to imprint the sequence of qualities for easy and active recall and involvement. According to traditional usage, this poem is recited in Jewish homes on Sabbath Eve by a husband to his wife, and before a wedding by the bridegroom to his bride.

By highlighting her skilful and righteous management of all aspects of a complex household, and her participation in physical labour, household tasks, trade, and the acquisition of property, the author presents the ʾēšet ḥayil as a character who provides leadership for the members of her domain and for all who would emulate her exemplary qualities. By specifying alphabetically her capabilities, talents, and virtues, the poet succeeds in painting a recognizable, but barely credible, portrait of a woman whose consistent and creative work is the source of the wealth, security, and status of her husband, children, and servants. While the human qualities of the ʾēšet ḥayil are stressed, the female imagery is highly idealized. As no human frailties are mentioned, the picture is that of an ideal woman/wife presented from a male perspective.

Coming as the conclusion to Proverbs, the poem with its carefully balanced structure, acrostic form, and hymn-like qualities, describes, in remarkably favourable terms, the ideal wife, recalls what is said about wives in the sentence literature, and recommends the ideal woman to unmarried men in the Israelite community. Most striking is the total focusing of Prov 31:10–31 on one female character who as wife and mother is one among many female figures in Proverbs.[23] This "woman who fears the Lord" (31:30) contrasts sharply with other female

---

23. In addition to the female characters in Prov 1–9, the book features many references to women, for example, "wife of your youth" (5:18); "neighbour's wife" (6:29); "good wife" (12:4; 31:10); "wife" (18:22); "wife's quarrelling" (19:13); "prudent wife" (19:14); "mother's teaching" (1:8; 6:20); and "mother" (4:3; 10:1; 15:20; 19:26; 20:20; 23:22,25; 28:24; 29:15; 30:11,17; 31:1).

figures in Proverbs, such as "the strange woman" (2:16; 5:3, 20a); "foreign /strange /alien woman" (5:20b; 6:24b; 23:27); "evil woman" (6:24a; 7:5); "foolish woman" (9:13); "beautiful woman without discretion" (11:22); "contentious woman" (25:24; 27:15); "woman dressed as a harlot" (7:10); and "harlot" (6:26; 23:27; 29:3). Female figures in Proverbs are dynamic and central, while often we hear little mention of husbands, fathers, or protectors. This poem functions as a summation of how a wise woman lives by portraying the main themes of Proverbs in the figure of the 'ēšet ḥayil.

Themes such as the importance of the acquisition of wisdom, the absolute contrasts between the wise and the foolish, the righteous and the wicked and their respective fates, the need to choose the right way, and the consequences of the choices made, all appear in this poem. It offers choices that are part of the larger and radical choice of Wisdom. A woman who surpasses all human expectations is presented as the concrete illustration of the blessing awaiting those who choose Wisdom and reject Folly. Simultaneously, it forms the climax of the book, and rounds it off by recalling a principal theme, the search for wisdom, outlined in Prov 1–9. Perhaps this closing section of the book of Proverbs is an epilogue. Its position ensures that readers see it as the culmination to the search for Wisdom advocated throughout Proverbs, while structurally it functions as an illuminating finale for the entire scroll.

In Prov 31:10, "Who can find a woman of worth?" (cf. 12:4; 18:22) highlights the rarity associated with the woman about to be described, while simultaneously reminding the audience of the search for Wisdom (Prov 1:22; 3:3; 4:22; 8:17, 35). This injunction also recalls that those who "find" her will be "happy" and they will find "life." Interestingly, "find" is used also to denote the adulteress's search, which, if successful, spells destruction for young men (7:15), whereas the "woman of worth" exemplifies the virtues lauded throughout Proverbs. If we read the book of Proverbs from beginning to end, it leads to the conclusion that to find the "woman of worth" one must search for Wisdom, avoid Folly, and become a faithful lover of Wisdom. Thus, we will find the unparalleled reward of the "woman of worth."

While the figure of Personified Wisdom in Proverbs is primarily a speaker in public places, at the city gates, in the streets, on the walls, by the road or path this is neither a feature of the 'ēšet ḥayil in Proverbs nor does it characterize Ruth. The 'ēšet ḥayil in Proverbs is a vivid and active, but idealized human figure, who speaks once "she opens her mouth with wisdom." Completing the picture of excellence is the reference to her care for the poor and needy (v. 20) who approach her at home. She is clothed in strength and dignity, speaks with wisdom and loving kindness (v. 26), and is proficient in all aspects of human life deemed essential by the author and his readers. The 'ēšet ḥayil is a wife and mother (v. 28) who spins, weaves, produces handcrafts, buys and sells, chooses and purchases land, plants a vineyard, trades in the market, imports food, and ensures adequate food supplies and warm clothing for her household throughout winter and works tirelessly. References to the woman's household, maids, spinning, weaving, buying and selling, her husband seated at the city gates, and her children, place her in the world of human beings. Her servants depend on her for nourishment, clothing, and daily tasks (vv. 15, 21, 27). She herself is never idle, as her lamp burns late into the night (vv. 13–15, 18, 27). A family portrait completes her embodiment as a female human being, with a husband and children, who sing her praises. A reflection on the reasons why she is worthy of praise brings the song to its conclusion: "Charm is deceitful, and beauty is vain, but a woman who fears the LORD is to be praised. Give her a share in the fruit of her hands, and let her works praise her in the city gates" (31:30–31).

At the beginning of Proverbs, a female figure, personified Wisdom, "cries out" at the entrance to the city gates (1:21) and in the final chapter the plea, "let her works praise her at the gates" (31:31), is made concerning the "woman of worth." Location, voice, and praise serve to unite the beginning and end of Proverbs as the voice of the female character, Wisdom, and the works of a female character, the "woman of worth," call for attention at the city gates, thus connecting personified Wisdom with the "woman of worth." The author/redactor of Proverbs has given us two distinct female characters. The location of the "valiant woman" in her home setting at the end of the book of Proverbs provides a clear clue to the esteem in which husband, children, household, community, and elders must hold such a woman in their midst. In addition, the author signals for the audience how "fear of the Lord" is central in the community. The woman of Worth who embodies the alphabetical list of the way of wisdom in everyday life is a highly idealized human figure. By positioning the poem at the end of Proverbs the author/redactor defines it as the final word, thus calling attention to its content and ensuring that the audience remembers it. We can envisage the final form of the book of Proverbs as a scroll that begins with the female figure of personified Wisdom, inviting those in public places to listen to her words (Prov 1:20–33) and concludes with another female figure, the human "woman of worth," who embodies a life lived according to wisdom.

Although Ruth is not at this stage wealthy or married with children (cf. Prov 31:22, 28), the overall theme of the woman who takes initiative inside and outside the household arena to provide for her family and for the needy is remarkably appropriate to the Ruth portrayed in the story so far. She "does good not harm" (Prov 31:12), she "works with willing hands" (1:13) and provides food for her household (31:15), "strength and dignity are her clothing" (31:25), "the teaching of kindness (*ḥesed*) is on her tongue" (31:26), "she does not eat the bread of idleness" (31:27), and "she fears the Lord" (31:30).

The meaning of the *NRSV* phrase "all the assembly of my people" is debated. The expression calls to mind the concluding phrase: "let her works praise her in the city gates" (Prov 31:31). It is easy to imagine based on what we know of Ruth so far that as Boaz's wife, she would become the epitome of the woman described in Prov 31. It is equally important to emphasize that so many key traits of the "woman of worth" are recognizable in Ruth quite apart from the context of marriage, children, and wealth presupposed in Prov 31. Her story serves as a balance and corrective to any cultural assumptions that only married women are truly "worthy."

Boaz's use of the term "woman of worth" is of further significance in its function as a feminine counterpart to the narrator's opening description of Boaz in 2:1 as *gibbôr ḥayil*.[24] Although Ruth is neither prominent nor rich, the appearance of the parallel expression collapses the social distance between them, while at the same time suggesting that Boaz is not only prominent and rich but is also thought to be morally worthy. He is one whose uprightness, fear of God, and diligence on behalf of family are admired in the community.[25]

One stunning contrast between the *'ēšet ḥayil* in Prov 31:16–18 "considers a field and buys; with the fruit of her hands she plants a vineyard" and the land transaction in Ruth 4:3 where neither Naomi nor Ruth has a say in the sale or transfer of the land: He then said to the next-of-kin, "Naomi, who has come back from the country of Moab, is selling the parcel of land that belonged to our kinsman Elimelech. As Boaz's lengthy reply continues in verses Ruth 3:12–13, he picks up Ruth's use of the next-of-kin redeemer terminology in a way that moves quickly beyond her general meaning in the direction of more technical legal usage. Boaz uses the Hebrew root five times and twice in verse 12, then three times in 3:13. His concern for ranking the order of importance of kinsmen and his insistence that this other man be given first option to exercise the right of next-of-kin fits with a legal approach rather than a general frame of reference. From the viewpoint of the story as a whole, Boaz can consider Ruth's words in a larger context anticipating consequences well beyond those she had in mind as she came to the threshing floor. Boaz's use of more technical redemption terminology points ahead to the final meeting at the town gate the next morning when he will introduce the issue of Naomi's parcel of land for sale (4:3). As he is aware of what the larger implications of Ruth's marriage would be, Boaz recognizes that Ruth's last act of loyalty to Naomi (the proposed marriage) will yield even greater benefits than Ruth anticipates. No wonder he invoked a blessing on her, and no wonder he has spoken of her reputation as a worthy woman. In his remarks about the situation concerning the next of kin, Boaz introduces two instructions to Ruth regarding her most immediate action.

Remain the night: Ruth 3:13–15

Boaz offers a double invitation to Ruth in 3:13, "remain this night," and concludes with "lie down until morning." Why this double instruction and the unwarranted course of action that prolongs their nocturnal meeting? Each of his two instructions reintroduces a verb loaded with significance from earlier in the narrative. The first *NRSV* "remain" is the same verb as "to lodge" that Ruth used in her words of commitment to Naomi (1:16). This is hardly casual considering the overall skill of the storyteller. Although the expression Boaz uses is a common one for spending the night, Ruth's lodging with Boaz until dawn anticipates her

---

24. *NRSV*: "prominent rich man."

25. A picture of Boaz has begun already to emerge in the events subsequent to 2:1 and will be fully confirmed by the end of the story.

lodging with Boaz in marriage. Yet her lodging with Boaz will not diminish her vow to Naomi. Ruth's commitment to Naomi is permanent. Boaz's instruction in effect specifies how Ruth is to spend the rest of the night with him. Here "rest" is the same as that used by Naomi (3:4) and the narrator (3:7–8) to describe the situation of Boaz and Ruth before this conversation. She is to lie down (maybe go to sleep)—the simple instruction steers clear of any suggestion of sexual activity. The reason for suggesting Ruth's staying for the night can only be guessed at. Boaz may have deemed it unsafe for Ruth to go out in the dark or conversely it might cast a shadow on his good name in the neighbourhood should someone recognize Ruth and gossip. Such a possibility would surely have cast some doubt on Boaz's uprightness. Ruth is a woman of worth and once more she must decide the wisest course of action for all concerned. While she appears to follow Boaz's instructions, she may also be doing what she deems will achieve her decision to indicate her willingness to stay with Boaz for life.

Three wisdom books (Proverbs, Ruth, and Song of Songs) in the Tanakh share some common themes, such as female perspectives on marriage, family, and sexuality. This canonical context lends considerable support to reading the book of Ruth as a wisdom text. Proverbs and Ruth are the only two books in the Bible that employ the phrase "woman/wife of strength/ worth/ substance," 'ēšet ḥayil (Prov 12:4; 31:10; Ruth 3:11). Boaz who is described with similar phraseology in Ruth 2:1 (ḥayil; cf., 4:11b) resembles the husband of Proverbs 31:23 who is respected at the city gates where he takes his seat among the elders of the land. When the book of Ruth is juxtaposed with Proverbs, one can easily appreciate the ways that the narrative presentation of Ruth and Boaz share many traits with Prov 31:10–31. A third reason to interpret Ruth as a wisdom text appears in the narrator's strategic choice of obscure words. In Ruth 4, it appears that the unique language that the author of Ruth uses, such as "acquiring *qanah* a wife" and acquiring the parcel of land (vv. 5, 10), may be possible allusions to the acquisition of wisdom (see Prov 4:5, 7; 16:16; 17:16; 23:23; cf., Prov 18:15). Therefore, Boaz not only acquires a wise wife but may also acquire wisdom itself. So, based on the canonical positioning of Ruth and the use of key terms and phrases like "woman/wife of noble character" and "acquire" in both Proverbs and Ruth, it is possible to read the book of Ruth as a wisdom text.[26]

Personification is not the only literary device employed in this poem. The poem is also chiastic, meaning that the segments in the first half correspond in reverse order to the segments in the second half. Such a link appears to connect with a central verse in the poem which stands alone: "Her husband is known in the city gates, taking his seat among the elders of the land" (v. 23). Prov 31:10–31 is an alphabetic acrostic. The initial letters of each verse form the complete Hebrew alphabet. One of the effects that the alphabetic acrostic form can have upon readers

---

26. As noted earlier, the Christian canons list Ruth between Judges and 1 Samuel, presumably because of the reference "In the days when the Judges ruled" (Ruth 1:1) and because of the genealogy in Ruth 4:18–22.

is the impression of comprehensiveness so that a poet covers the subject from A to Z. The book of Proverbs concludes with this poem that reviews and illustrates the teachings of wisdom with a feminine metaphor. While the "wife of noble character" and personified wisdom herself are more valuable than rubies (Prov 3:15; 8:11; 31:10). The woman of worth exhibits fulfilment, prosperity, balance, and justice.

The man who marries an industrious woman is an ideal man of worth who choses wisely by embracing wisdom. Prov 2:6 shows that God is the source of wisdom, and Prov 8:22–31 teaches that wisdom preceded the creation of the world (see also Prov 3:19–20; Job 28:23–27). Wisdom literature repeatedly commends "the fear of the Lord" (Prov 9:10; 15:33; Job 28:28; Eccl 12:13). So it is not surprising that the book of Proverbs opens (Prov 1:7) and closes with reference to the fear of the Lord.

Boaz pronounces the blessing of YHWH on Ruth, lauds her for not pursuing younger men, and tells her that the assembly of his people know that she is *'ēšet ḥayil*, "a woman of worth" or valiant woman. One might ask how Boaz, a land-owning male Israelite, and his assembly of male elders decide that Ruth was a *'ēšet ḥayil*, a woman of worth. A third consideration is how does the description of Ruth as *'ēšet ḥayil* function today to challenge some notions of women as the property of male family members, or of those to whom they are married, or as chattels in a large household where they may not seek change, and their family members perceive them as incapable of caring for themselves and their children?

In biblical texts, the Hebrew word *ḥayil* usually appears in descriptions of male characters as in *'is ḥayil* to denote a warrior, a man of valour, courage, one strong in battle, powerful, and unafraid. *Ḥayil* as a descriptor of female characters appears only in Ruth 3:11, Prov 12:4, and Prov 31:10–31. In Prov 31:10–31, *'ēšet ḥayil* is usually translated as "a capable," "perfect," and "good" wife, a valiant woman, "a woman of worth," or "a woman of substance." As "woman" and "wife" share the one word, they are interchangeable in Hebrew, as they are in many languages. Ruth and the Woman in Prov 31 share several of the same characteristics and differ in many more. The rare use of *ḥayil* to describe these female characters suggests that they are exceptional. It seems incredible that Ruth, a Moabite widow and recent immigrant, had become known as a "woman of worth" in Bethlehem in a seemingly very brief time.

Chapter 7

RUTH: EARTH'S VOICE

A close ecological reading of the book of Ruth reveals that Earth and Earth elements play leading roles throughout the narrative. Traditionally, many scholars have read this story as a narrative about human loyalty and the _ḥesed_ of two women. However, Earth's voice and Earth's actions are paramount from the opening verses announcing famine and its accompaniments that drive Elimelech's family into exile in Moab right to the concluding genealogy (4:18–22) that lauds Earth's voice throughout history.

Ruth 1:1–5: Famine, exile, and death

Famine, a reversible Earth action, drives the decision of Elimelech, Naomi, and their sons, Mahlon and Chilion, to leave their home in Bethlehem and go as hungry exiles to Moab where they hoped to find sustenance and shelter. Death, an irreversible Earth action, first claims Elimelech. The possibility of new life surfaces with the news that the two sons, Mahlon and Chilion, take Moabite wives, Orpah and Ruth. They live in Moab for ten years (Ruth 1:4). This fleeting promise of new life vanishes when we hear that both sons die. Earth's irreversible and destructive actions take centre stage in 1:1–2 with famine, which listeners know accompanies crop failure, hunger, starvation, and exile for the family of Elimelech and Naomi. Death and sterility stalk Naomi's ten-year stay in Moab. Death takes Elimelech, Mahlon, and Chilion, leaving Naomi, Ruth, and Orpah childless widows with all three men interred in the Earth of Moab. Naomi's move to Moab also meant that she left behind any support she might have received had she remained in Bethlehem. Thus, death, one of Earth's irreversible acts, ends three marriages and the hope of a new life. Exile, bereavement, barrenness, loss, and death, as outlined in Ruth 1:1–5, suggest a story without a future.[1]

---

1. But the deaths of Elimelech, Mahlon, and Chilion at the story's beginning is counterbalanced at the end by the conception and birth—Earth actions—of a son who holds the promise of future life and survival, not only for human survivors at the centre of the narrative but for their descendants also (4:14–17).

Ruth 1:6–13: Return to Bethlehem

A sharp contrast to the preceding five verses appears in "Then she started to return with her daughters-in-law from the country of Moab, for she had heard in the country of Moab that the LORD had considered his people and given them food." Naomi's decision to return to the land of Judah indicates how Earth's voice calls Naomi from Moab with the news that "the Lord has considered his people and given them food." The use of the alliterative phrase *lāté lāhem lāhem* suggests a happy chant accompanying joyful news. It is also the first of two references to the Lord's direct intervention in human life.[2] In this case, the news of Earth's fruitfulness precedes and prompts human decisions and actions. Naomi said to her two daughters-in-law, "Go back each of you to your mother's house. May the LORD deal kindly with you, as you have dealt with the dead and with me" (1:8).

Naomi's instructions to her daughters-in-law envisage marriage as the only possible security for women (1:11–13). Her words express hopeless despair and self-pity, mixed with altruistic concern. "Would you then refrain from marrying? No, my daughters, it has been far more bitter for me than for you, because the hand of the LORD has turned against me" (Ruth 1:13). Naomi's ambivalence emerges in her instructions to Ruth and Orpah. Whether she is expressing genuine concern for their future or rejection of her widowed daughters-in-law, she instructs them to return to the homes of their mothers. Naomi does not envisage an independent existence for Ruth or Orpah as she cannot provide husbands for them. Ruth responds with an Earth-centred vow, pledging to accompany Naomi: "Do not press me to leave you or to turn back from following you! Where you go, I will go; where you lodge, I will lodge; your people shall be my people, and your God my God. Where you die, I will die—there will I be buried. May the LORD do thus and so to me, and more as well, if even death parts me from you!" (1:16–17).

Ruth 1:18–22: Naomi's lament

When Naomi saw that she was determined to go with her, she said no more to her. So the two of them went on until they came to Bethlehem. When they came to Bethlehem, the whole town was stirred because of them; and the women said, "Is this Naomi?" She said to them, "Call me no longer Naomi, call me Mara, for the Almighty, has dealt bitterly with me. I went away full, but the LORD has brought me back empty; why call me Naomi when the LORD has dealt harshly with me, and the Almighty has brought calamity upon me?" So Naomi returned together with Ruth the Moabite, her daughter-in-law, who came back with her from the country of Moab. They came to Bethlehem at the beginning of the barley harvest.

---

2. In both instances, the narrator portrays the Lord as acting to secure a future, first by the provision of food and second by enabling the conception of a child (4:13).

Ruth 1:18–22 portray Naomi's perception of how the Lord has treated her. She defines "full" and "empty" in verse 21 solely in terms of male relatives, while overlooking the fact that she with her household left for Moab, not "full" but fleeing from famine. Ten years later, she is returning to Bethlehem having suffered the loss of husband and sons but assured by Ruth's vow of loyalty to her, to her God, and her land. Auspiciously, the two women's arrival in Bethlehem coincides with the beginning of the barley harvest. Verse 22 alerts readers to Earth's voice and actions in the harvests, and the promise of the season's fruitfulness. Coupled with this situation is a reminder of the control that Earth's voice and Earth's activities have over the lives of the human characters. From an Earth perspective, Ruth 1:1–22 moves from famine to harvest, from Bethlehem to Moab, and back to Bethlehem. Throughout these verses, Ruth's actions and decisions are Earth-directed and Earth-dependent.[3] Naomi, on the other hand, acts and speaks as if she is at odds with Earth and lacks hope for a fruitful return home to Bethlehem even with the prospect of food and a plentiful harvest. From an ecological perspective, Earth's voice announces a movement from the emptiness of famine, hunger, exile and death to the fullness of a fruitful harvest of grain. Earth's voice and Earth's actions are consistently ahead of all human sequences.

Ruth 2:1–7: Earth provides food, protection, and acceptance

Chapter 2 opens with the narrator introducing Boaz. Ruth offers to work as a gleaner: "Now Naomi had a kinsman on her husband's side, a prominent rich man, of the family of Elimelech, whose name was Boaz." Ruth the Moabite said to Naomi, "Let me go to the field and glean among the ears of grain, behind someone in whose sight I may find favour" (2:1–2). Ruth still called a Moabite, hopes that she will find a field where she will glean some grain (barley) to feed Naomi and herself. Here she claims the right of the poor enshrined in Torah to glean at harvest time (Lev 19:9–10). The narrator attributes her arrival in Boaz's field to chance/luck (*miqreh*). Boaz's question to his servant, "To whom does this young woman belong?" reflects the assumptions of a patriarchal society and one that identifies human beings by their place of origin and family ties. The servant identifies Ruth not by name but as a Moabite and by her relationship to Naomi. However, he also mentions her unstinting labour, her stamina, and perseverance: "without resting even for a moment [*NRSV*] or 'she has been on her feet ever since she came this morning' [*JSB*] she has hardly had a moment's rest in the shelter." Ruth's fellow

---

3. Pathos and irony pervade this chapter—despite Ruth's extraordinary vow of loyalty to Naomi and her God, and her choosing a future of uncertainty but her vow to Naomi binds the two women. Naomi seems to ignore her as do the people of Bethlehem. The narrator says, "Naomi returned and Ruth the Moabite" (1:22). Ruth's identification with and trust in Earth means she can rely on the Earth of Bethlehem to sustain her life and Naomi's from this point forward.

workers recognize and laud Ruth's closeness to Earth and her ability to "be on her feet" to be one with Earth as she gleaned.

Ruth 2:8–23: Ruth identifies with Earth and Earth's fruits

In Ruth's first encounter with Boaz, he commands her to remain in his field and offers her protection and advice (2:9).[4] His invitation highlights the fruits of Earth that he offers Ruth: "When you are thirsty go to the vessels and drink what the young men have drawn." Then she fell prostrate, with her face to the ground/Earth (*Eretz*), and said to him, "Why have I found favour in your sight, that you should take notice of me when I am a foreigner?" (2:10). The combining of the Lord's blessing and Boaz's favour is significant as is his claim "under whose wings you have sought refuge" (2:12–13). At mealtime, Boaz invites Ruth to eat some bread and dip her morsel in the wine, and he passed her parched grain. She ate until she was satisfied and had some leftovers for Naomi. Only the Lord can pay her wages in full "full reward," but Boaz is to be the agent of this blessing for under his skirts (*kanap*) Ruth will eventually find security (3:9). Earth's fruitful harvest makes possible Boaz's generous provision of grain to Ruth and Naomi.

Ruth knows how to obtain the best from her labour in Boaz's field because she is one with Earth. She gleaned in the field until evening, and then beat out what she had gleaned, and took it back to Naomi in the city along with her leftover lunch! The narrator now covers an extended period of gleaning by Ruth with: "She stayed close to the young women of Boaz, gleaning until the end of the barley and wheat harvests; and she lived with her mother-in-law" (2:23). Ruth's gleaning in Boaz's field provided the grain that relieves the two women's physical hunger. The fullness provided by the soil of Ruth's new land is a prelude to the fulfilment of Naomi's more abiding need of security for herself and Ruth.

Ruth 3:1–8: Naomi plots and Ruth cooperates

The conclusion of the grain harvests heralds an uncertain future for Ruth and Naomi. Where will they find sustenance now? Naomi takes the initiative with a cunning plan for a long-term solution to their precarious existence. Chapter 3:1–3 opens with Naomi speaking to Ruth: "My daughter, I need to seek some security for you, so that it may be well with you. Now here is our kinsman Boaz, with whose young women you have been working. See, he is winnowing barley tonight

---

4. Boaz's protection of Ruth (v. 9), "I have ordered the young men not to molest you," contains echoes of the divine protection afforded to Sarah (Gen 20:6) and Rebecca (Gen 26:11). Ruth's response plays on the verb "acknowledge" and the noun "foreigner" (*nokri*), a category of persons distinct from the "resident alien" (*ger*) who had legal rights of protection within the community.

at the threshing floor." Following Naomi's instructions about how to prepare for her encounter with Boaz on the threshing floor, Ruth went down to the threshing floor in the darkness and observed where he went to lie down at the end of the heap of grain. Then she came stealthily, uncovered his feet, and lay down on the Earth close to Boaz.

Ruth 3:13–18: Ruth modifies Naomi's plan

At midnight, the man was startled and behold a woman lay at his feet (3:8). He said, "Who are you?" She answered, "I am Ruth, your servant; spread your cloak over your servant, for you are next-of-kin." He said, "May you be blessed by the LORD, my daughter; this last instance of your loyalty is better than the first; you have not gone after young men, whether poor or rich … my daughter, do not be afraid, I will do for you all that you ask, for all the assembly of my people know that you are a woman of substance. But now, though it is true that I am a near kinsman, there is another kinsman more closely related than I" (3:9–12). Boaz use of the term *eshet hayil* (woman of substance/worth) for Ruth inevitably evokes the woman in Prov 31:10–31 and calls up the stunning female figure that closes the book of Proverbs. As Boaz continues speaking to Ruth, he says "do not be afraid" which reminds readers how significant a risk Ruth has taken in approaching him by night and making her proposal. He could have taken advantage of her physically or rebuffed her proposal. He could have compromised her integrity, letting the village know about the episode. Boaz's agreement to her request and his assertion about her excellent reputation confirms his awareness of her reasons to be afraid. His description of Ruth's reputation in the community as that of a "woman of worth/substance," *'ēšet ḥayil*, calls to mind another appearance of this rare phrase in the introduction to the description of the kind of woman to be desired as a wife[5] (Prov 31:10). Although Ruth is not at this stage wealthy or married with children or in a position to buy land, plant a vineyard, produce handicrafts and sell them in the market, or have servants (cf. Prov 31:22, 28). The *'ēšet ḥayil* of Proverbs takes the initiative inside and outside the household to provide for her family. Her portrait is remarkably appropriate to Ruth portrayed in the story so far. She "does good not harm" (Prov 31:12); she "works with willing hands" (1:13) and provides food for her household (31:15); "strength and dignity are her clothing" (31:25); "the teaching of kindness (*hesed*) is on her tongue" (31:26); "she does not eat the bread of idleness" (31:27); and "she fears the Lord" (31:30). The possibility of intertextual allusion to Prov 31 is supported by a second unusual expression used in the same sentence with *'ēšet ḥayil*.[6] Based on what we know of Ruth so far, it is

---

5. *NRSV* "capable wife."

6. The *NRSV* phrase "all the assembly of my people" is more literally translated as "all the gate of my people." Although its technical meaning is debated, this expression calls to mind the concluding phrase from the lengthy description of the capable wife: "let her works praise her in the city gates" (Prov 31:31).

easy to imagine that as Boaz's wife she would become the epitome of the woman described in Prov 31. However, it is equally important to emphasize that so many key traits of the "woman of substance" in Proverbs are recognizable in Ruth quite apart from the context of marriage, children, and wealth presupposed in Prov 31. Her story so far serves as a balance and corrective to any cultural assumption that only married women are indeed "worthy."

Boaz's use of the term 'ēšet ḥayil is of further significance in its function as a feminine counterpart to the narrator's opening description of Boaz in 2:1 as gibbôr ḥayil.[7] While Ruth is neither prominent nor wealthy, the appearance of the parallel expression collapses the social distance between them, while at the same time suggesting that Boaz is not only prominent and wealthy but is also thought to be morally worthy, one whom the community admires for his uprightness, fear of God, and diligence on behalf of family. This admirable picture of Boaz has begun to emerge in the events after 2:1 and readers see it confirmed by the end of the story.

As Boaz's lengthy reply continues in 3:12–13, he picks up Ruth's use of the next-of-kin redeemer terminology in a way that moves quickly beyond her general meaning in the direction of a more technical legal practise. He uses the Hebrew root five times and twice in verse 12, then three times in verse 13. His concern for ranking the order of importance here, and his insistence that this other man receives first option to exercise the right of next of kin, fits with a right approach rather than a general frame of reference. From the viewpoint of the story as a whole, Boaz can consider Ruth's words in a broader context anticipating consequences well beyond those she had in mind as she went to the threshing floor. His more technical use of redemption terminology points ahead to the meeting at the town gate the next morning when he will introduce the issue of Naomi's parcel of land that is for sale (4:3).

Because he is aware of the broader implications of Ruth's marriage, Boaz recognizes that Ruth's last act of loyalty to Naomi (the proposed marriage) will yield even more significant benefits than Ruth anticipates. Little wonder that his invoked blessing on her spoke of her reputation as a "woman of worth." Boaz also introduces two instructions to Ruth beginning with "remain this night" and concluding with "lie down until morning." Why this double instruction and the risky course of action that prolongs the nocturnal encounter? Each of his two instructions reintroduces a verb loaded with significance from earlier in the narrative. The first "remain" is the same verb as "to lodge" that Ruth used in her commitment to Naomi (1:16). Surely, this occurrence is not accidental on the part of the narrator who displays considerable skill in storytelling. Although the expression Boaz uses is a common one for spending the night, Ruth's lodging with Boaz this night anticipates her lodging with Boaz in marriage. However, her lodging with Boaz will not diminish her vow to Naomi, whom she continues to

---

7. *NRSV* "prominent rich man."

regard as most in need of her *ḥeseḏ*. Ruth's commitment to Naomi is more reliable and permanent. Boaz's instruction in effect specifies how Ruth is to spend the rest of the night with him. Here "rest" is the same word as that used by Naomi (3:4) and the narrator (3:7–8) to describe the situation of Boaz and Ruth before this conversation. She is to lie down. Boaz's reason for suggesting Ruth's stay the night is open to conjecture. Should Ruth go out in the darkness she would have no protection and would also have drawn attention to her journey. Boaz's uprightness may also have come into question.

Once more Earth provides—the darkness of night enables and witnesses the resolution of famine and provides the means of survival with the scene played out at the threshing floor amidst piles of harvested grain when a vulnerable foreign widow enters a dangerous place as a supplicant. Earth supplies the threshing of new grain, formation of new relationships, and in time the generation of new life. Earth's actions enable newfound relationships with Earth, with the Earth community, and the human sphere. Earth's gift of darkness and silence enables human actions to take place in secret, thus avoiding problems of disclosure and gossip and acknowledging that the success of human actions and decisions in the Ruth narrative depend on Earth's provision of night and day and Ruth's willingness to undertake a dangerous journey in thick darkness.

Despite the allusion to a nearer next of kin who may be a potential obstacle, Boaz presses on and invites Ruth to "remain this night, and in the morning if he will act as next-of-kin for you, good; let him do it. If he is not willing to act as next-of-kin for you I will act as next-of-kin for you" (3:11–14). This element of uncertainty hints that Naomi's cunningly conceived plan requires luck and Earth to work in Ruth's favour: "Wait, my daughter, until you learn how the matter turns out, for the man will not rest, but will settle the matter today" (3:18). Interestingly Naomi does not invoke Divine assistance here when it seems that it might be the only solution to this dilemma. The emphasis on waiting evokes the waiting required for seeds to germinate in the soil and flourish if there is to be a fruitful harvest. As with Ruth's secret entry to the threshing floor in the darkness, she exits from the threshing floor under cover of darkness once more utilizing Earth's gift of the night. Dawn illumines Ruth's emergence with a generous supply of grain provided by Boaz, perhaps signalling that Naomi's strategy will bring to birth her fondest hope—the birth of a new generation through the union of Ruth and Boaz.

Ruth 4:1–10: Boaz secures land and Ruth a husband

Chapter 4 opens as follows: "No sooner had Boaz gone up to the gate and sat down there than the next-of-kin, of whom Boaz had spoken, came passing by." So Boaz invited him to sit. Then Boaz took ten men of the elders of the city and said, "Sit down here"; so, they sat down. Boaz said to the next of kin, "Naomi, who has come back from the country of Moab, is selling the parcel of land that belonged to our kinsman Elimelech. So I thought I would tell you of it and say: Buy it in the presence of those sitting here, and in the presence of the elders of my people. If you will redeem it, redeem it; but if you will not, tell me, so that I may know; for there is no one prior to you to redeem it, and I come after you." So he said, "I will redeem it." Then, Boaz mentions a snag. "The day you acquire the field from the hand of Naomi, you are also acquiring Ruth the Moabite, the widow of the dead man, to maintain the dead man's name on his inheritance." At this, the next of kin said, "I cannot redeem it for myself without damaging my own inheritance. Take my right of redemption yourself, for I cannot redeem it."[8] Then, Boaz said to the elders and all the people, "Today you are witnesses that I have acquired from the hand of Naomi all that belonged to Elimelech and all that belonged to Chilion and Mahlon. I have also acquired Ruth the Moabite, the wife of Mahlon, to be my wife, to maintain the dead man's name on his inheritance, in order that the name of the dead may not be cut off from his kindred and from the gate of his native place; today you are witnesses."

Ruth 4:11–13: Blessing and genealogy

Then all the people who were at the gate, along with the elders, said, "We are witnesses. May the LORD make the woman who is coming into your house like Rachel and Leah, who together built up the house of Israel. May you produce children in Ephrathah and bestow a name in Bethlehem; and, through the children that the LORD will give you by this young woman, may your house be like the house of Perez, whom Tamar bore to Judah." So, Boaz took Ruth and she became his wife. When they came together, the LORD made her conceive, and she bore a son. Now for the second time in the Ruth narrative, the Lord intervenes to enable Ruth to conceive.

Ruth 4:14–17: Women of Bethlehem bless Naomi

"Blessed be the LORD, who has not left you this day without next-of-kin; and may his name be renowned in Israel! He shall be to you a restorer of life and a nourisher of your old age; for your daughter-in-law who loves you, who is more to you than seven sons, has borne him." This blessing recalls the disaster that led to Naomi's good fortune in meeting Ruth in Moab. Such looking back to the beginning of the narrative highlights the place of chance in life over which humans have no control and reflects how Earth and Earth's elements provide or withhold Earth's fruits.

8. Now this was the custom in former times in Israel concerning redeeming and exchanging: to confirm a transaction, the one took off a sandal and gave it to the other; this was the manner of attesting in Israel. So when the next of kin said to Boaz, "Acquire it for yourself," he took off his sandal.

Ruth 4:18–22: Concluding genealogy

In the concluding genealogy (4:18–22), the women of Bethlehem pray that Ruth, identified as "the woman/wife coming into your house," will fulfil a similar role to that of Rachel and Leah. These two wives of the ancestor Jacob "built up the house of Israel" by bearing between them eight of the twelve sons remembered as progenitors of the twelve tribes of Israel. Significantly, the blessing in 4:1 compares Ruth to Rachel and Leah, mothers to the twelve tribes, whereas 4:12 associates Ruth with Tamar. She, like Ruth, was a foreigner who by unconventional means secured the future of a life threatened by extinction (Gen 38).[9] Boaz arranges the ratification of the agreement concerning the field and the marriage.

Ruth 4:18–22 concludes the Ruth narrative. Like most genealogies in the Old Testament, it does not list any non-Israelites or any women. In these final verses of the narrative, the characters cease to speak, and the narrator concludes, "Now these are the descendants of Perez: Perez became the father of Hezron, Hezron of Ram, Ram of Amminadab, Amminadab of Nahshon, Nahshon of Salmon, Salmon of Boaz, Boaz of Obed, Obed of Jesse, and Jesse of David."

Amid starvation and famine in Bethlehem, the book of Ruth began with a patriarchal framework, three men and one woman; Elimelech decided to take his family to Moab. In 4:18–22, the narrator returns readers to a traditional patriarchal conclusion, documenting the family line of David and recording the births of several fathers remembered in the tradition. From 4:14 to the conclusion of the narrative in 4:22, Ruth is not active in the narrative. "Then Naomi took the child and laid him in her bosom and became his nurse." The women of the neighbourhood gave him a name, saying, "A son has been born to Naomi." They named him Obed; he became the father of Jesse, the father of David.[10] The story ends with Naomi surrounded by the women of Bethlehem celebrating the birth of Obed, a male child and the future grandfather of David. Ruth 4:17–22 may be a condensed genealogy. It connects David back to Obed, with further verses developing the genealogy and restating significant elements. Repetition may have been integral to foundational accounts as biblical narratives often repeat essential knowledge—Bethlehem, Moabite, male parentage, and related details. However, one could also imagine a process of textual expansion of original story conclusions as later generations desire more substantial and locally based narratives.

9. Ruth is not the first foreign woman to enter the genealogy of the Davidic line.

10. Ruth 4:18–22: Now, these are the descendants of Perez: Perez became the father of Hezron, Hezron of Ram, Ram of Amminadab, Amminadab of Nahshon, Nahshon of Salmon, Salmon of Boaz, Boaz of Obed, Obed of Jesse, and Jesse of David. Matt 1:1–20 provides a long account of the genealogy of Jesus the Messiah, the son of David, the son of Abraham with Jacob the father of Joseph the husband of Mary, of whom Jesus was born, who is called the Messiah; Luke traces Jesus back to Adam.

Koosed notes that genealogies appear throughout the *Tanakh*, but they usually begin rather than end stories, for example, 1 Sam 1:1; Esth 2:5; 1 Chr 1–9.[11] Gen 5 traces the descendants of Noah's three sons, Shem, Ham, and Japheth, by their families, their languages, their lands, and their nations. Gen 10:32 notes, "These are the families of Noah's sons, according to their genealogies, in their nations; and from these, the nations spread abroad on the Earth after the flood." 1 Chr 1–9 contains the most extended biblical genealogy, tracing humankind from Adam through all the families of the twelve tribes of Israel. The first Book of Chronicles repeats with slight expansion most of the genealogy found in Ruth 4:18–22.[12]

Insofar as Ruth 4:18–22 comprises a genealogy, it is in the traditional male format, father to son. Many present-day readers would expect the father's and mother's names to appear. However, the names of the women who bore the descendants do not appear. A Jewish friend explained this practice as follows: "Everyone in the community knew who the mother was as she bore and raised her children, and she could vouch for the child's paternity. Traditionally communities accepted a mother's word for her progeny's paternity."[13]

The genealogy begins with the descendants of Perez who is the son of Tamar. It continues through to Boaz, the husband of Ruth; Obed, the son of Ruth; Jesse, the grandson of Ruth; and David, the great, great-grandson of Ruth. While the genealogy does not mention either Tamar or Ruth, the genealogy could not exist without these women. The Bible highlights the importance of lineage for the continuation of the Israelite people, whose genealogies invariably portray the people as descended from a long line of ancestors united under a covenant with YHWH, the God of Israel. Whether or not all the names listed in the genealogies are historical personalities, cumulatively they represent the past of a people while connecting the present community with their ancestors. Genealogies function as chains connecting one significant period or series of events to another. Often, they are long and consist mostly of names that contain few, if any, identifying features.[14] They also tie the descendants to their land and their ancestry.

11. Jennifer Koosed, *Gleaning Ruth: A Biblical Heroine and Her Afterlives* (Columbia: University of South Carolina Press, 2011), 120. Matt 1:1–17 traces Jesus ancestry back to Abraham; Luke traces Jesus back to Adam.

12. Edward F. Campbell, *Ruth, AB 7* (New York: Doubleday, 1996), 70. Campbell notes that the opening of the Ruth genealogy is like those in Gen 5 and 10 and Num 3:1. It also corresponds to the contents of the genealogy of 1 and 2 Chr.

13. My Jewish friend wishes to remain anonymous but asks that this information to be included here.

14. This is true also of New Testament genealogies. In tracing Jesus back to Adam (and to God Luke 3:23–38) or tracing forward from Abraham to Jesus (Matt 1:2–16), the goal is to provide a pedigree for Jesus. The OT provides no information about some of the names of men and therefore readers of the Bible know nothing about them. Whereas Jews read the genealogies as part of annual or triennial Torah readings, Christians rarely read the OT genealogies at their liturgies.

The final five verses of Ruth are a case in point. While the author references some names elsewhere in the Bible, others appear only here. All we know is that the person is a place marker between the man who preceded him and the man who followed, as part of the same family line. This picture of Boaz begins to emerge in the events after 2:1, and the narrator verifies them by the end of the story. "Through the children that the LORD will give you by this young woman, may your house be like the house of Perez, whom Tamar bore to Judah."[13] So Boaz took Ruth, and she became his wife. When they came together, the Lord made her conceive, and she bore a son (Ruth 4:12). Boaz's concern with levirate marriage and the keeping of property in the family may not stem from uniquely legal concerns but may reflect a fundamental cultural value and a norm that was widespread at the time. He then said to the next of kin, "Naomi, who has come back from the country of Moab, is selling the parcel of land that belonged to our kinsman Elimelech … The day you acquire the field from the hand of Naomi, you are also acquiring Ruth the Moabite, the widow of the dead man, to maintain the dead man's name on his inheritance" (4:4–5). The *JPS Tanakh* translation of 4:5 places a question mark at the end of that verse. This translation changes the intention of the verse and clears up any legal questions on the topic. If one assumes that Boaz is asking a question here, he is not stating some assumed legal requirement but is asking the *goʾel* what his intentions are. Boaz implies that the acquisition of Ruth as a wife is of necessity tied to the redemption of Elimelech's field. According to biblical law, levirate marriage pertained only to the brother of the dead husband (Deut 25:5–10). For this reason, neither Boaz nor the other *Goʾel* is legally bound to marry Ruth. Biblical law did not link marriage with the redemption of the land. Nevertheless, the narrator and other characters accept the link articulated by Ruth on the threshing floor as a fundamental premise. Boaz says to the *Goʾel*, "You said you are willing to buy the field, but do you intend to marry Ruth as well?" The first *Goʾel* opts out.

The dialogue on the threshing floor regarding respective identities points up some significant considerations. Boaz said, "Who are you?" She answered, "I am Ruth, your servant; spread your cloak over your servant, for you are next-of-kin." 3:9 suggests that Ruth presumes Boaz to be in the position of *Goʾel*, as he is not a brother of Mahlon, Ruth's deceased husband. Boaz clarifies his relationship with "though I am indeed a near relative, there is another relative more closely related than I" (3:12). The term *Goʾel* is a legal one, and it focuses mainly on the preservation of family and community. Generally, it did not include marital obligations towards widows. The Ruth narrative associates the term *Goʾel* with rights and responsibilities affecting marriage in cases where the law of levirate marriage required a man to marry his brother's widow to perpetuate the family line. However, levirate laws do not refer to *Goʾel*. Only in the book of Ruth is marriage among kin and land redemption linked. The narrative suggests that Ruth accepts the situation. Once Ruth and Boaz marry, and Ruth gives birth to Obed, both she and Naomi vanish from the narrative. Many glorify the fact that Ruth gives birth to a son and regard this event as legitimating her acceptance in her new land with her mother-in-law and the relatives of her two husbands, one deceased and one living.

Beyond the context of the era of the Judges, the story of Ruth reaches back to the story of the birth of Perez (Gen 38, cf. Ruth 4:12, 18). The narrator goes back further to Rachel and Leah (4:11), thus giving Ruth a place of honour alongside the classic mothers of Israel. Reaching ahead, the story connects with King David (indirectly 1:1–2; directly in 4:17, 18–22).[15] Despite multiple direct and indirect allusions to other Bible texts outside the book of Ruth, the only other reference to the Ruth story is within the Christian canon in the genealogy in Matt 1:5. Here Ruth is one of four women alongside Tamar, mother of Perez, Rahab, and the "wife of Uriah" who are in a list of forty-two generations of male ancestors of Joseph, the husband of Mary, of whom Jesus was born (Matt 1:16). Scholars are unanimous in claiming that the choice of these four women was not random.

Old Testament tradition presumes that three of the women mentioned were non-Israelite (Gentiles); later traditions also regarded the fourth, Tamar, as non-Israelite. Narrators usually indicated that all four women's stories included undesirable sexual activity and dubious marriage circumstances. Rahab's problematic involvement is her occupation as a prostitute while hiding the Israelite spies (Josh 2:1), which does not raise questions about her place in the genealogy.[16] The connection has nothing to do with irregular sexual activity. These four women do not fit neatly into either the category of Gentiles or the category of women having questionable sexual encounters with the fathers of their offspring. Still, the names of these women may anticipate Matthew's interest in including Gentiles and probably may hint that Jesus unusual birth was not a matter of concern. Ancestors' ethnicity and sexual histories may not have been the only or exclusive concern in genealogies in the ancient world as ultimately the storytellers had to accept mothers' words for the veracity of their accounts of the paternity of their children. Many scholars argue that 4:18–22 are an appendix to the Ruth narrative and not an original part of it.[17] However, Adele Berlin investigated the poetic function of these verses and concluded that the genealogy was not an addition but an essential part of the narrative.[18] She noted the characters and events in Ruth are

15. The concluding genealogy in Ruth appears in a more segmented format in 1 Chr 2:5–16.

16. Marshall D. Johnson, *The Purpose of the Biblical Genealogies, with Special Reference to the Setting of the Genealogies of Jesus*, 2nd ed. (Cambridge: Cambridge University Press, 1988), 162–65. Matthew's identification of the Canaanite Rahab as Boaz's mother does not appear anywhere in any extant Hebrew tradition. The Matthean genealogy probably included Rahab by extrapolation from a documented tradition that Rahab was a member of the tribe of Judah.

17. See Campbell, 172; Jeremy Schipper, *Ruth: A New Translation with Introduction and Commentary*, AYBRL 7D (New Haven, CT: Yale University Press, 2016), 186. Jack M. Sasson, *Ruth: A New Translation with a Philological Commentary and a Formalist-Folklorist Interpretation* (Sheffield: Sheffield Academic Press, 1995), 178–87.

18. Adele Berlin, *Poetics and Interpretation of Biblical Narrative* (Sheffield: Sheffield Almond Press, 1994 [1983]), 110.

independent of the characters and events from Genesis to Kings and argues that in Ruth, the genealogy situates the characters and events among a group of familiar characters. The author highlights Boaz as seventh in the genealogy, Perez, Hezron, Ram, Amminadab, Nahshon, Salmon, and Boaz. Alternatively, this genealogy might have been inserted to create a link between an independent account and a more comprehensive list of characters. Above all, genealogies serve to locate characters as Earth people who belong in specific geographic locations. Thus, they are portrayed as part of the land and its history and have left descendants who have permanent ties to the ancestors and their line.

Earth and Earth elements have the final word

Following three chapters where the narrator focuses consistently on Earth elements and the strength and robust decision making of females, Ruth 4 raises surprising situations that demand consideration. First, among these are the male-centred legal proceedings at the gate and the male-focused blessing addressed to Boaz. One might find this as a counterpoint to the women-centred closing scene (4:18–22). Seriously concerning is a presumption that a satisfactory social structure depends on a male heir and economic arrangements that include financial support provided by a wealthy husband. According to the narrative, Ruth needed a male *go'el*. However, the response of the women to Naomi in 4:15, "He shall be to you a restorer of life and a nourisher of your old age; for your daughter-in-law who loves you, who is more to you than seven sons, has borne him," raises doubts about the importance of sons to the women of Bethlehem. However if, as the women claim, Ruth's love for Naomi is of more value than seven sons, why does the narrative focus on Naomi and Obed? The final conundrum arises from the concluding genealogy which is male while the scroll bears Ruth's name.

From a tale of famine, exile, loss, death, and recovery, the genealogy points to a glorious future. In the canonical context, their importance lies in giving the story a broader significance than the purely domestic and in introducing the promise of hope after the despair with which the book of Judges ends. An ecological reading of Ruth offers the audience a vision of the wholeness of Earth and the Earth community. Ruth's simplicity and attractiveness as a human story mask the pivotal roles that famine, day, night, land, fields, barley harvest, wheat harvest, and threshing floor play in the narrative. The narrator depicts each of these Earth elements, accomplishing its purpose in the Earth community. We realize how each human character is totally at the mercy of these Earth elements. In the course of the narrative, some human characters live, and some die. The narrator embodies in the experience of each of the human characters a contrast between death and life and offers examples of what it means to "choose life" (Deut 30:11–20). The flourishing or decline of Earth and the Earth community highlights the absolute dependence of human creatures on Earth and all its elements.

An ecological interpretation enables readers to recognize the story's embodiment of a this-worldly hope sustained by a narrator who invites readers to identify with

Earth, and Earth's creatures, in a struggle for survival. While the geographic locale and genealogy relate to David, the explicit focus of the narrative is concerned with Earth's actions rather than with divine actions. Many have argued that the Ruth narrative highlights how the decisions of two female characters embody and bring to pass the blessings of God in this narrative. Such readings subordinate the role of Boaz to the activities of Ruth and Naomi. By highlighting the human aspect of the action, many opt to focus on how the female characters escape destitution and starvation and find life and prosperity. Such readings must address Earth, and all of Earth's elements that enable and support the human characters. Some see women as wringing concessions and opportunities out of the dominant male, patriarchal setting in which they live. Economic security often masks female economic dependence and a flourishing patriarchal system that relies on the practice of *ḥeseḏ* to make up for poor distribution and sharing of Earth's resources.

Hermeneutic of suspicion

A story that many have read as a text that highlights women's power to bring fulfilment and human liberation calls for a "hermeneutic of suspicion." As the Ruth story develops, the focus is on Earth's voice, elements, and actions. Ruth is a narrative in which Earth, Earth characters, and human actors are involved and resist consideration under the single viewpoint of the omniscient narrator. There is a continuing struggle to find a way through apparent hermeneutical impasses, not only regarding the Ruth text but also regarding scripture generally. As many scholars assert, most Bible texts are products of patriarchal cultures. "Patriarchal" does not refer solely to male-female relationships but also include the complexity of interacting hierarchies of race, class, religion, and ethnicity that rely on or support intricate power patterns.

The Ruth story may be read as supporting a societal structure in which the narrative links women's economic security to marriage, preferably to a rich man. Some readers question Ruth's devotion to her mother-in-law, thus making Ruth an ideal daughter-in-law. In some instances, church leaders and male pastors have used this story to urge women to accept roles in families that may reduce them to servitude. For such women, Ruth becomes an oppressive text portraying a community characterized by the image of women bound by cultural, economic, and social structures. When the women of Bethlehem say, "A son has been born to Naomi" (4:17), many hear what an indication of unclear or unjust inheritance structures are hidden here. Many may sense that this expression supports a cultural tradition that they resist. Some regard the joyful climax of the book as abhorrent.

A first step in reclaiming the voice and actions of Earth and Earth elements in the Ruth narrative is a rejection of the notion that the narrative is essentially and solely about the human characters. A hermeneutical move to an Earth reading demands recognition of some critical features in this text. These assume specific understandings of the relationships with Earth and Earth elements of the human characters in the text. Like many ancient narratives, the text has been invoked to sanctify family and cultural structures or to reinforce traditional patterns of economic dependence in marriage. From an ecological perspective, the Ruth story exhibits a human community characterized by reciprocal relationships with Earth and Earth elements. The Ruth narrative portrays human characters who recognize their dependence on Earth and Earth's produce. Today, humans must also accept that our survival demands racial and ethnic inclusiveness and enable all creatures to enjoy Earth's resources. The Ruth story functions as a microcosmic drama in which Earth, Earth elements, and creatures enable Earth's voice to sound and echo throughout the narrative. Earth elements, such as crop failure or success, fruitful or failed harvests, fertile land or depleted land, plentiful food and work, and many other Earth products, play critical roles for all creatures. The village scale of the vision, while microcosmic and thus more readily imaginable, is not of lesser significance because of its scale.

Sustenance, inclusiveness, justice, care for all, cherishing of all life on a global scale, and a willingness to accept that Earth's resources are not infinite is integral to an Earth-focused vision for the future. The particularity of such a microcosmic image may lead scholars to see various culturally specific inadequacies of the vision. While it may be appropriate to question practices past or present as failing to embody Earth concerns, it is also essential to avoid making absolute Earth readings of this text. The story of Ruth could not exist without human participants in the sense that the actions of the characters, most notably Ruth, Boaz, Naomi, and other men and women of Bethlehem, provide engaging characters that move the action along. In reading intentionally from an Earth perspective, interpreters' focus not only encompasses the notion of God working with Earth and all Earth's creatures including the human characters but also highlights how all Earth elements participate in and heed Earth's voice in a fruitful search as they seek for Earthly harmony.

Because of the traditionally anthropocentric bias of Bible texts and biblical interpreters and scholars, our tendency to read from anthropocentric viewpoints demands considerable effort to place Earth and Earth elements as central and pivotal rather than supposing some cataclysmic divine action to effect radical transformation in the text.

God language in Ruth

Many have emphasized that biblical language about God is metaphorical but widespread adherence to referring to the Deity as a male continues. While many will agree that God is not "male," but this fundamental starting point for appropriating God language has consequences for our interpretation of texts from an ecological perspective. Once the opening verses establish the disastrous situation of famine, flight, and death, the remainder of the story highlights just two direct interventions of God towards the restoration of wholeness and community. God's provision of food in a formerly famine-stricken Bethlehem (1:6) initiates the restoration as does the narrator's attribution of Obed's conception to the Deity

(4:13). The two divine acts attributed to the Deity in Ruth may represent those aspects of the natural order over which ancient peoples experienced the least control. Elsewhere in Ruth, human beings call on God to do what they believe themselves unable to accomplish as we see in Naomi's prayer in Ruth 1:8 to Ruth and Orpah: "Go back each of you to your mother's house. May the LORD deal kindly with you, as you have dealt with the dead and with me."

The text suggests that God is at work behind human actions, all of which are inseparable from Earth's ongoing momentum as experienced in the absence or failure of water sources, crop failure, infertility, and total famine. Likewise plentiful rainfall and dew water ensure a fertile land and fruitful harvests that yield abundance of grains, wine, oil, fruits, vegetables, and ultimately life or death.

Inherent in the narrative is an implied message that humans do not have to choose between God's action and human endeavours. The Ruth story does not present great powers of sin and evil as obstacles the characters must overcome, but they do have to confront the power of hunger, famine, death, the battle for scarce resources, and possible prejudice against outsiders. Ruth begins, "In the days of the Judges there was a famine in the land." This era we know from the book of Judges as one filled not only with Israelite warfare against external enemies but also with the most horrific internal struggles, murders, and destruction imaginable, devastation in which women were especially victimized (Judg 19–21). Over against such communal collapse, Ruth offers a narrative for a different way, watched over by God and initiated through an unexpected human source—a woman, a poor widow, a foreigner, a poverty-stricken gleaner, a Moabite.

CONCLUSION

This study of the biblical book of Ruth from an Earth perspective considers the power of this short story to transcend geographical and historical boundaries by speaking to all concerned about the plight of our Earth. The narrative is self-contained and focuses primarily on the development of plot and characters. Thematically, the narrative highlights emigration and immigration and successful residence in an alien land. Thus, it brings together Israelite and foreign cultures and shows a range of different attitudes in Israel to foreigners, with the insistence that important human relations are possible across ethnic boundaries.

Ruth portrays a Moabite widow among Israelites. The problems addressed by the narrator affect many more than those named in the narrative. The action of the story perpetuates a family line that might have died out, but for some lucky decision made by Ruth. These eventuate in the birth of Obed, the grandfather of the great ancestor David whose great-grandmother is a Moabite. The narrator uses history-like details and plot devices to illustrate how Ruth and Naomi handle a law-based society and authority. A motif of obtaining food is significant as is the linking of the main character with the city gate (Ruth 4:1).

Central to this study is a recognition of the non-human as legitimate determining factors in the progress of the narrative. Several anthropocentric biases emerge throughout the narrative and are discussed at several points throughout this commentary. This study sought to recognize Earth and members of the Earth community as valid characters in the narrative. I sought to give voice to the way in which Earth and members of the Earth community function throughout the story.

Integral to my reading of the text was concern for members of the Earth community, for domains of Earth such as food, famine, death, harvests, day and night, and darkness and light. By identifying with non-human characters and earthy elements in the narrative, I could read the text of Ruth with new eyes.

Thematically, the narrative outlines a story about a family and those who become part of the family through the course of the narrative and in so doing uncovers for readers aspects of the world of ancient Israel and introduces readers to some of the characters' values and customs. A famine causes the family to emigrate from Bethlehem and to immigrate to the neighbouring Moab where they live for ten years. There the two sons marry Moabite women, but during their stay in Moab the father, Elimelech, and sons, Malon and Chilion, die.

On hearing that the Lord had given food to the people of Bethlehem, Naomi decides to return to Bethlehem, her home. Orpah, Chilion's Moabite wife, remains in Moab as advised by Naomi but contrary to Naomi's advice, Ruth emigrates from Moab and accompanies Naomi to Bethlehem. The narrator vividly recounts Ruth's vow to Naomi: "Where you go, I will go; where you lodge, I will lodge; your people shall be my people, and your God my God. Where you die, I will die—there will I be buried. May the LORD do thus and so to me, and more as well, if even death parts me from you!" (Ruth 1:16–17). Ruth's willingness to marry Naomi's next of kin may be a broad-minded understanding of the Levirate law in order to provide a son for her deceased husband to preserve the family line but likely to be influenced by the desperate need to find security for both women.

In the face of hardship and loss, Ruth and Naomi display extraordinary courage. They trust Earth and Earth's agency. They exhibit perseverance, ingenuity, and are willing risk-takers. All three widows, Naomi, Ruth, and Orpah, made life-defying decisions that they would have known might jeopardize their futures and the present and future lives of others.

Boaz is the quintessential wealthy male who also expresses concrete acts of loving kindness as he responds to the two widows who connive to obtain his help.

It is hoped that readers today become conscious of Earth's gifts and elements and identify with the characters in this book who recognize and treasure Earth, Earth's elements, and Earth's creatures. Famine, natural disasters, and war may be direct causes for the displacement.

Insights from Ruth studies mentioned in footnotes and in the bibliography, and insights from others working in the field of Earth Bible commentaries, enrich interpretations and challenges. Many have challenged accepted interpretations of Ruth.

I aimed to offer some understandings from contemporary studies of Ruth. This study leads me to conclude that while for some the book of Ruth can be read as endorsing the stereotyping that a woman's happiness is dependent on marriage and motherhood, it does not have to be. Rather, I believe that we could read Ruth as portraying a strong and independent woman who took responsibility for her own actions, decisions, and future as well as her past. She lived loving kindness and was an agent of her own history and the history of the people of Israel.

An Earth reading of the Ruth text has opened new and important understandings and ways of interpreting the text. My aim to read the text from an Earth perspective revealed to me liberating challenges. I hope other readers also find the diverse insights expressed in these pages helpful in the journey towards understanding of how Earth and Earth creatures and elements enlarge perceptions of integration, and inclusion. Viewing the text through an Earth lens enables readers to take an inclusive and liberating stance.

In order to read Ruth from an Earth perspective and reclaim the place of Earth and all its elements in the Ruth narrative, one must reject the notion that the narrative is solely about the human characters. This way of reading means that we do not read this text from an ancient place and time, or only as a village story. Instead, we note how the human characters relate to Earth and its elements.

Such a reading of Ruth offers a vision of the wholeness of Earth and of the Earth community. It enables readers to realize how each human character is totally at the mercy of Earth and Earth's elements. The narrator focuses on the actions of Earth and Earth's elements such as famine, exile, death, barley and wheat harvests, land ownership, day and night, rather than concentrating on the contributions of the Deity to a favourable resolution of the story.

Ruth 4:12, "shall be to you a restorer to life and a nourisher of your old age for your daughter-in-law who loves you who is more to you than seven sons has borne him," may support a view that the women of Bethlehem are evaluating the relative importance of males and females both for Naomi and those gathered at the town gate. At this point, the narrative builds towards the significance of a male redeemer and a male heir. A genealogy that does not include any female ancestors seems ridiculous. Surprisingly, the naming of the scroll the Megillah of Ruth—is this the final punchline as the scroll bears Ruth's name?

By seeking to interpret Ruth from an Earth perspective, readers may recognize the story's embodiment of a this-worldly hope sustained by a narrator who invites his/her audience to identify with Earth, and Earth's creatures, in the struggle for survival. Ruth is a narrative in which Earth, Earth characters, and human actors are involved and resist consideration under the single viewpoint of an omniscient narrator. An Earth reading of Ruth raises questions about how we interpret the relationships of the human characters with one another, with Earth, and with the Earth community.

BIBLIOGRAPHY

Aschkenasy, Nehama. *Woman at the Window: Biblical Tales of Oppression and Escape.* Detroit, MI: Wayne State University Press, 1998.

Avnery, Orit. "Who Is In and Who Is Out: The Two Voices of Ruth." *HAVRUTA* no. 3 (2010). Accessed September 26, 2019.

Beattie, D. R. G. "Ruth 3." *Journal for the Study of the Old Testament* 5 (1978): 39–48.

Bergant, Dianne. "Ruth: The Migrant Who Saved the People." *Wiley Online Library* 18, no. 2 (2003): 49–61.

Berlin, Adele. *Poetics and Interpretation of Biblical Narrative.* Sheffield: Sheffield Almond Press, 1994 [1983].

Berquist, Jon L. "Role Differentiation in the Book of Ruth." *JSOT* 57 (1993): 23–37.

Berquist, Jon L. "Resistance and Accommodation in the Persian Empire." In *In the Shadow of Empire: Reclaiming the Bible as a History of Faithful Resistance,* edited by Richard A. Horsley, 41–58. Louisville, KY: Westminster John Knox, 2008.

Birch, Bruce C. "Walter Brueggemann." In *A Theological Introduction to the Old Testament,* 2nd ed., edited by Terence E. Fretheim and David L. Petersen. Nashville, TN: Abingdon Press, 2005.

Black, James. "Ruth in the Dark: Folktale, Law and Creative Ambiguity in the Old Testament." *Literature and Theology* 5 (1991): 20–36.

Brenner, Athalya. "Naomi and Ruth." *VT* 33 (1983): 385–97.

Brown, Francis, S. R Driver, and Charles A. Briggs. *BDB.* Peabody, MA: Hendrickson, 1996.

Bush, Frederic W. *Ruth-Esther,* WBC. Dallas, TX: Word Books, 1996.

Campbell, Edward F. *Ruth: A New Translation with Introduction and Commentary.* Anchor Bible Garden City, NY: Doubleday, 1975.

Carmody, D. L. *Biblical Woman: Contemporary Reflections on Biblical Texts.* New York: Crossroad, 1988.

Caspi, Mishael. *The Book of Ruth: An Annotated Bibliography.* New York: Garland, 1994.

Chittister, Joan D. *The Story of Ruth: Twelve Moments in Every Woman's Life.* Grand Rapids, MI: Eerdmans, 2000.

Chu, Julie L. C. "Returning Home: The Inspiration of the Role Dedifferentiation in the Book of Ruth for Taiwanese Women." *Semeia* 78 (1998): 47–53.

Dube, Musa W. "Divining Ruth for International Relations." In *Other Ways of Reading: African Women and the Bible,* edited by Musa W Dube, 179–98. Atlanta, GA: Society of Biblical Literature, 2001.

Eskenazi, Tamara, and Tikva Frymer-Kensky. *JPS Bible Commentary: Ruth.* Philadelphia, PA: Jewish Publication Society of America, 2011.

Farmer, Kathleen A. Robertson. "The Book of Ruth." In *The New Interpreter's Bible: Numbers—Samuel,* edited by Leander E. Keck, 2, 891–946. Nashville, TN: Abingdon Press, 1998.

Fewell, Danna N., and David M. Gunn. "A Son is Born to Naomi." *JSOT* 40 (1988): 99–108.

Fewell, Danna N., and David M. Gunn. "Boaz, Pillar of Society: Measures of Worth in the Book of Ruth." *JSOT* 45 (1989): 45–59.

Fewell, Danna Nolan, and David M. Gunn. *Compromising Redemption: Relating Characters in the Book of Ruth.* Louisville, TN: Westminster John Knox, 1990.

Fisch, Harold. "Ruth and the Structure of Covenant History." *VT* 32 (1982): 425–37.

Fischer, Irmtraud. *Rut.* HTKAT. Freiburg: Herder, 2001.

Fontaine, Carol R. "Ruth." In *The Women's Bible Commentary*, edited by Carol A. Newsom and Sharon H. Ringe, 145–52. Louisville, TN: Westminster, 1992.

Frymer-Kensky, Tikva. *Reading the Women of the Bible: A New Interpretation of Their Stories.* New York: Schocken Books, 2002.

Gafney, W. "Ruth." In *The Africana Bible: Reading Israel's Scriptures from Africa and the African Diaspora*, edited by H. Page, 249–54. Minneapolis, MN: Fortress, 2010.

Gaventa, Beverley Roberts. *Mary: Glimpses of the Mother of Jesus*, Studies on Personalities of the New Testament. Columbia: Columbia University of South Carolina Press, 1995.

Goh, Elaine W. F. "An Intertextual Reading of Ruth and Proverbs 31:10–31 with a Chinese Woman's Perspective." In *Reading Ruth in Asia*, edited by Sione Havea and Peter H. W Lau, IVBS 7, 73–88. Atlanta, GA: SBL Press, 2015.

Grant, Reg. "Literary Structure in the Book of Ruth." *Bibliotheca Sacra* 148 (1991): 424–41.

Gray, John. *Joshua, Judges, Ruth*, New Century Bible Commentary. Grand Rapids, MI: Eerdmans, 1986.

Haag, Herbert, Dorothee Solle, Katharina Elliger, Marianne Grohmann, Helen Schungel-Straumann, and Christoph Wetzel. *Great Couples of the Bible.* Minneapolis, MN: Fortress Press, 2006.

Habel, Norman C. *Readings from the Perspective of Earth.* Vol. 1 Earth Bible, edited by Normal C. Habel. Sheffield: Sheffield Academic Press, 2000.

Hiebert, Paula S. "Whence Shall Help Come to Me? The Biblical Widow." In *Gender and Difference*, edited by Peggy L. Day, 125–41. Minneapolis, MN: Fortress, 1989.

Holladay, Carl R. "Contemporary Methods of Reading the Bible." In *NIB*, edited by Leander E. Keck, 125–49. Nashville: Abingdon, 1994.

Hubbard, Anthony. *The Book of Ruth*, NICOT. Grand Rapids, MI: Eerdmans, 1989.

Johnson, Marshall D. *The Purpose of the Biblical Genealogies, with Special Reference to the Setting of the Genealogies of Jesus*, 2nd ed. Cambridge: Cambridge University Press, 1988.

Kates, Judith A., and Gail T. Reimer. *Reading Ruth: Contemporary Women Reclaim a Sacred Text.* New York: Ballentine, 1994.

Koosed, Jennifer. *Gleaning Ruth: A Biblical Heroine and Her Afterlives*, Studies on Personalities of the Old Testament. Columbia: University of South Carolina Press, 2011.

LaCocque, André. *The Feminine Unconventional*, Overtures to Biblical Theology. Minneapolis, MN: Fortress Press, 1990.

LaCocque, André. *Ruth: A Continental Commentary.* Translated by H. C. Hanson. Minneapolis, MN: Fortress Press, 2004.

Laffey, Alice L., and Mahri Leonard-Fleckman. *Ruth: Wisdom Commentary.* Vol. 8, edited by Barbara E. Reid. Collegeville, MN: Liturgical Press, 2017.

Lapsley, Jacqueline E. *Whispering the Word: Hearing Women's Stories in the Old testament.* Louisville, KY: Westminster John Knox, 2005.

Lau, Peter H. W. *Identity and Ethics in the Book of Ruth: A Social Identity Approach*, BZAW. Gottingen: De Gruyter, 2010.

Levine, Amy-Jill. "Ruth." In *Women's Bible Commentary*, edited by Carol A. Newsom and Sharon H. Ringe, 85–90. Louisville, KY: Westminster John Knox, 1998.

Linafelt, Tod, and Timothy K. Beal. *Ruth & Esther*, Berit Olam. Collegeville, PA: Liturgical Press, 1999.

Mangrum, Ben. "Bringing 'Fullness' to Naomi: Centripetal Nationalism in the Book of Ruth." *HBT* 33, no. 1 (2011): 62–81.

Masenya, Madipoane. "Ngwetši (Bride): The Naomi-Ruth Story from an African-South African Woman's Perspective." *Journal of Feminist Studies in Religion* 14, no. 2 (1998): 81–90.

Masenya, Madipoane. "A Commentary on the Book of Ruth." In *Global Bible Commentary*, edited by D. Patte, 86–91. Abingdon: Nashville, 2004.

Masenya, Madipoane. *How Worthy Is the Woman of Worth? Rereading Proverbs 31:10–31 in African-South Africa*. New York: Peter Lang, 2004.

Masenya, Madipoane. "Struggling with Poverty/Emptiness. Rereading the Naomi-Ruth Story in African South Africa." *Journal of Theology in Southern Africa* 120 (2004): 46–59.

Masenya, Madipoane. "Seeking Security through Marriage: Ruth1:6–18 Placed under an African Woman's HIV and AIDS Lens." *Journal of Constructive Theology* 13, no. 2 (2007): 43–56.

Matthews, Victor H. *Judges and Ruth*. Cambridge: Cambridge University Press, 2004.

Matthews, Victor H. "The Determination of Social Identity in the Story of Ruth." *BTB* 30 (2006): 49–54.

McKinlay, Judith E. "A Son Is Born to Naomi: A Harvest for Israel." In *A Feminist Companion to Ruth and Esther*, edited by Athalya Brenner, 151–57. Sheffield: Sheffield Academic Press, 1999.

Meyers, Carol. "To Her Mother's House: Considering a Counterpart to the Israelite Bêt'âb." In *The Bible and the Politics of Exegesis: Essays in Honor of Norman K. Gottwald on His Sixty-Fifth Birthday*, edited by D. Jobling, P. L. Day, and G. T. Sheppard, 39–52. Cleveland, OH: Pilgrim Press, 1991.

Miller, Patrick D. *The Way of the Lord: Essays in Old Testament Theology*, 1st ed. Grand Rapids, MI: Eerdmans, 2007.

Mills, Mary E. *Biblical Morality: Moral Perspectives in Old Testament Narratives*. Aldershot: Ashgate, 2001.

Moore, Michael B. "To King or Not to King: A Canonical-Historical Approach to Ruth." *BBR* 11 (2001): 27–41.

Moore, Michael S. "Ruth the Moabite and the Blessing of Foreigners." *Catholic Biblical Quarterly* 60, no. 2 (1998): 203–17.

Nadar, Sarojini. "A South African Indian Womanist Reading of the Character of Ruth." In *Other ways of Reading: African Women and the Bible*, edited by Musa W. Dube, 159–75. Atlanta, GA: SBL, 2001.

Nielsen, Kirsten. *Ruth: A Commentary*. Translated by Edward Broadbridge, OTL. Louisville, KY: Westminster John Knox, 1997.

Olson, Mark J. "Pentecost." In *Anchor Bible Dictionary*, edited by D. N. Freedman, 5, 222–23. New York: Doubleday, 1992.

Patrick, Dale, and Allen Scult. *Rhetoric and Biblical Interpretation*, 1st ed. JSOTSup. Sheffield: Sheffield Academic Press, 2009.

Powell, Stephanie Day. *Narrative Desire and the Book of Ruth*, The Library of Hebrew Bible/Old Testament Studies, Playing the Texts. London: T&T Clark, 2018.

Rauber, D. F. "Literary Values in the Bible: The Book of Ruth." *JBL* 89 (1970): 27–37.

Rosaldo, M. Z. "Women, Culture, and Society: A Theoretical Overview." In *Women, Culture, and Society*, edited by M. Z. Rosaldo and L. Lamphere, 17–42. Stanford, CA: Stanford University Press, 1974.

Russell, Letty M. *The Future of Partnership*. Philadelphia, PA: Westminster Press, 1979.

Russell, Letty M. "Authority and the Challenge of Feminist Interpretation." In *Feminist Interpretation of the Bible*, edited by Letty Russell, 139. Philadelphia, PA: Westminster Press, 1985.

Russell, Letty M. *Household of Freedom: Authority in Feminist Theology*. Philadelphia, PA: Westminster John Knox, 1987.

Sakenfeld, Katharine D. *The Meaning of Hesed in the Hebrew Bible: A New Inquiry*. Vol. 17, HSM. Missoula, MT: Scholars Press, 1978.

Sakenfeld, Katharine D. *Faithfulness in Action*. Philadelphia, PA: Fortress Press, 1985.

Sakenfeld, Katharine D. *Compromising Redemption: Relating Characters in the Book of Ruth*. Louisville, KY: Westminster/John Knox Press, 1990.

Sakenfeld, Katharine D. "At the Threshing Floor: Sex, Reader Response, and a Hermeneutic of Survival." *Old Testament Essays* 15, no. 1 (2002): 164–78.

Sasson, Jack M. *Ruth: A New Translation with a Philological Commentary and a Formalist-Folklorist Interpretation*. Baltimore, MD: John Hopkins University Press, 1979.

Sasson, Jack M. "Ruth." In *The Literary Guide to the Bible*, edited by Robert Alter and Frank Kermode, 321–28. Cambridge: Harvard University Press, 1987.

Sasson, Jack M. *Ruth: A New Translation with a Philological Commentary and a Formalist-Folklorist Interpretation*, 2nd ed. Sheffield: Sheffield Academic, 1995.

Say Pa, Anna May. "Reading Ruth 3:1–8 from an Asian Woman's Perspective." In *Engaging the Bible in a Gendered World: An Introduction to Feminist Biblical Interpretation in Honor of Katharine Doob Sakenfeld*, edited by Linda Day and C. Pressler, 47–59. Louisville, KY: Westminster John Knox, 2006.

Schipper, Jeremy. *Ruth: A New Translation with Introduction and Commentary*, AYBRL 7D. New Haven, CT: Yale University Press, 2016.

Schüssler-Fiorenza, Elisabeth. *But She Said: Feminist Practices of Biblical Interpretation*. Boston, MA: Beacon Press, 1992.

Shalev-Eyni, Sarit. "In the Days of the Barley Harvest: The Iconography of Ruth." *Artibus Et Historiae* 26, no. 51 (2005): 37–57.

Sölle, Dorothee, Joe H. Kirchberger, and Herbert Haag. *Great Women of the Bible in Art and Literature*. Grand Rapids, MI: Eerdmans, 2006.

Strouse, Evelyn, and Bezalel Porten. "A Reading of Ruth." *Commentary* 67/2 (1979): 64–67.

Tiessen, Nathan. "A Theology of Ruth: The Dialectic of Countertestimony and Core Testimony." *Direction: A Mennonite Brethren Forum* 39, no. 2 (Fall 2010): 255–64.

Toy, Crawford H. *A Critical and Exegetical Commentary of the Book of Proverbs*, ICC. Edinburgh: T & T Clark, 1899.

Trible, Phyllis. "Ruth." In *ABD*, edited by D. N. Freedman, 5, 842–47. New York: Doubleday, 1992.

van Dijk-Hemmes, Fokkelein. "Ruth: A Product of Women's Culture?" In *A Feminist Companion to Ruth*, edited by Athalya Brenner. Sheffield: Sheffield Academic Press, 1993.

Weems, R. J. *Just a Sister Away: A Womanist Vision of Women's Relationships in the Bible*. San Diego, CA: LuraMedia, 1998.

Wenham, Gordon J. *Story as Torah: Reading the Old Testament Ethically*. Edinburgh: T & T Clark, 2000.

Westermann, Claus. "Structure and Intention of the Book of Ruth." *Word and World* XIX, no. 3 (Summer 1999): 285–302.

Whyte, M. K. *The Status of Women in Pre-Industrial Societies.* Princeton, NJ: Princeton University Press, 1978.

Wolde, Ellen J. van. "Texts in Dialogue with Texts: Intertextuality in the Ruth and Tamar Narratives." *Biblical Interpretation* 5 (1997): 1–28.

Yee, Gale A. "'She Stood in Tears amid the Alien Corn': Ruth, the Perpetual Foreigner and Model Minority." In *They Were All in One Place? Toward Minority Biblical Criticism,* edited by R. C. Bailey, 119–40. Atlanta, GA: SBL, 2009.

Zevit, Ziony. "Dating Ruth: Legal, Linguistic and Historical Observations." *ZAW* 117 (2005): 574–600.

AUTHOR INDEX

SUBJECT INDEX

BIBLICAL INDEX